TRIUMPH
B O O K S

BEARCAT MURRAY
FROM OL' POTLICKER TO CALGARY FLAMES LEGEND

Jim "Bearcat" Murray
with George Johnson

TRIUMPH
BOOKS

Copyright © 2021 by Jim Murray and George Johnson

No part of this publication may be reproduced, stored in a retrieval system, or transmitted in any form by any means, electronic, mechanical, photocopying, or otherwise, without the prior written permission of the publisher, Triumph Books LLC, 814 North Franklin Street, Chicago, Illinois 60610.

Library of Congress Cataloging-in-Publication Data

Names: Murray, Jim, 1933 January 2- author. | Johnson, George, 1957- author.
Title: Bearcat Murray : from ol' potlicker to Calgary Flames legend / Jim "Bearcat" Murray ; with George Johnson.
Description: Chicago, Illinois : Triumph Books, 2021.
Identifiers: LCCN 2021028489 | ISBN 9781629379142 (paperback) | ISBN 9781641257060 (epub)
Subjects: LCSH: Murray, Jim, 1933 January 2- | Calgary Flames (Hockey team)—History. | Athletic trainers—Alberta—Calgary—Biography. | BISAC: SPORTS & RECREATION / Winter Sports / Hockey | TRAVEL / Canada / Western Provinces (AB, BC)
Classification: LCC GV848.C25 M87 2021 | DDC 796.092 [B]—dc23
LC record available at https://lccn.loc.gov/2021028489

This book is available in quantity at special discounts for your group or organization. For further information, contact:
Triumph Books LLC
814 North Franklin Street
Chicago, Illinois 60610
(312) 337-0747
www.triumphbooks.com

Printed in U.S.A.
ISBN: 978-1-62937-914-2
Design by Patricia Frey
Page production by Nord Compo
Photos courtesy of the Murray family

I really cannot thank my family—my better half, Shirley; oldest son, Allan, and his boys, Jesse and James; youngest son, Danny; his wife, Michele; and their son, Spencer—enough for supporting me through the years and being such a big part of this story.

—Bearcat

CONTENTS

FOREWORD *by Lanny McDonald*   ix

INTRODUCTION *by George Johnson*   xi

CHAPTER 1.   One Night in Montreal...   1

CHAPTER 2.   Beginnings   7

CHAPTER 3.   The Cowboy Way   19

CHAPTER 4.   Getting into the Business   25

CHAPTER 5.   The Professional Ranks   41

CHAPTER 6.   The Big Apple and Cowtown   55

CHAPTER 7.   Move to the Dome   77

CHAPTER 8.   The Rise: Battle Lines Drawn,
               March to the Finals   83

CHAPTER 9.   The Push in '89   103

CHAPTER 10.   The Fall   115

CHAPTER 11.   Trick of the Trade   121

CHAPTER 12.   Behind the Curtain   127

CHAPTER 13.   Stepping Away   133

CHAPTER 14.   Rivals/Friends   143

CHAPTER 15.   Shangri-La   151

CHAPTER 16.   A Bearcat Q&A   157

CHAPTER 17.   Snapshots   179

CHAPTER 18.   The Fraternity   217

CHAPTER 19.   Family   227

CHAPTER 20.   Charity Work   237

CHAPTER 21.   Call from the Hall   247

CHAPTER 22.   Being Bearcat   253

CHAPTER 23.   As the Seconds Ticked Away...   265

ACKNOWLEDGMENTS   273

FOREWORD

I WAS 15 YEARS OLD the first time I met the larger-than-life energy that is Bearcat Murray.

I was a bright-eyed teenager walking into the Calgary Centennials training camp in the summer of 1968, and I declared to the trainer, "Hi, my name is Lanny, and I'm here to play hockey."

With a strong handshake, a signature smile, and a mischievous twinkle in his eye, Bearcat laughed and said, "Well, good for you, kid!"

Just like that, we were instant friends.

My story is not unique—there's not a player who's worked with ol' Pot who doesn't have that same instant connection.

It was always rewarding through my junior career with the Medicine Hat Tigers to visit with Bearcat after the games in Calgary; and when I was traded to the Flames years later, he made it an even warmer homecoming.

With the stature of a jockey but the size of a lion, Bear's energy could only be described as infectious, vibrating. He had this way of pumping you up just by being around him. A man who could never sit still, he played every shift, with every player, bobbing and swaying on the bench; the seventh man on the ice.

His celebrity status preceded him in places like Boston or New York, where he was the only NHL trainer to my knowledge to have his own fan club. Groups of fans would show up in his likeness—bald head and big moustache—and chant his name from the stands. We would rib him in the dressing room for being the real superstar on the team, but he loved it.

In the same sentence, Bear could be defined as both old-school and ahead of his time. He inconspicuously saw and heard everything and responded accordingly.

He knew the big picture, the relationships, every side conversation, the quiet self-doubt and the attempts to hide pain—and somehow knew how to show up for every member of the team in exactly the way we needed. He knew our strengths better than we did, and quietly bolstered our weaknesses with words of encouragement or a kick in the butt to get your chin up, if that's what was required.

Bearcat epitomized the mark of any good trainer—the glue that holds it all together.

He never missed a thing.

I owe Bearcat a lot for being the kind of trainer he was—a father figure, a mentor, a confidant, and my biggest advocate and cheerleader, right up until my final game.

I caught his quiet eyes peeking around the corner when I learned I would play in Game 6 in the 1989 Final, and heard him scurry off and let out a signature "YIP!" in the dressing room. We won the Stanley Cup that night. He told us we would months before. Of course he believed it before we did.

One of my most cherished photos from that night is of me lifting Bearcat off his feet on the ice, our joy pouring out of the picture. I remember yelling: "We did it!"

We...

I'm confident it wouldn't have happened without him.

Lanny McDonald played more than 1,100 games in the NHL and co-captained the Calgary Flames to a Stanely Cup championship in 1988–89. McDonald was inducted into the Hockey Hall of Fame in 1992 and now serves as the chair of its board of directors.

INTRODUCTION

THE EXACT YEAR HAS BEEN MISLAID somewhere in the mists of legend.

The details, happily, have not.

One memorable night down at the Saddledome, his Highness Prince Albert Alexandre Louis Pierre Grimaldi II, then heir to the throne of the Principality of Monaco and only son of Hollywood royalty Grace Kelly, is visiting Calgary in order to train at the Olympic bobsleigh track at Canada Olympic Park.

He waits patiently to be introduced to the local celebrity.

The local celebrity, the short, balding man with a thick bushy moustache and twinkling eyes, is busy shaking hands. Lots of hands.

In the confusion, he doesn't quite catch the name of his famous guest.

Something, obviously, has gotten lost in translation.

"How ya doin'? Name's Bearcat Murray," the local celebrity blurts, extending his hand to an astonished prince.

"I've got friends in Prince Albert. Colder 'n hell up there!"

Now a spry 88 and every iota as famous, as recognizable, as he was those countless game nights down through all those winters inside the rustic old Calgary Corral followed by the state-of-the-art Saddledome and other arenas far afield, trainer Jim "Bearcat" Murray has carved for himself an extraordinary niche.

"He's just one of those characters, those unforgettable personalities, that you're lucky enough to find in the game," praised longtime Flames play-by-play man Peter Maher. "There are so many Bearcat stories, you lose track; you don't know where to begin."

Murray himself continues to be confounded by all the fuss.

"It's incredible," he concedes. "I don't understand it. I go to Calgary, to a function, I walk in, and for a lot of people it's 1989 again. Everybody wants to shake my hand. Everybody knows me. I don't know why. I just shake my head. My dad, if he was here, would say: 'Jimmy, it's just… mind-boggling!' That was one of his favourite sayings. I can still hear him say it: '…mind-boggling!'

"But it is. People still recognize you, make a fuss over you. I truly, truly do not understand why. But it's heart-warming, let me tell you.

"I've been one lucky little potlicker."

Bearcat sharpened his first skate at age 12. Rode as a jockey on the bush-league thoroughbred circuit. Wildcatted in the oil fields and, launching himself into the career that would take him to places and moments he could never have dreamt of, worked as a self-taught trainer for the junior Centennials and Wranglers, the World Hockey Association's Calgary Cowboys, and the Canadian Football League's Calgary Stampeders.

Most famously, in 15 years tending bruises, cuts, missing teeth, and other assorted injuries for the big team in the oil-and-gas town, the NHL's Calgary Flames, he transformed himself without any conscious effort into an authentic legend around the city, the province, an instantly recognizable figure throughout the entire NHL, forever at the ready with a smile or handy with a yarn.

He's one of those rare people who instantly makes others feel good, feel comfortable, feel somehow a part of it all.

Also known far and wide as Lil' Potlicker, he's the only trainer in pro sports who can claim his own fan club—two, to be exact, one chapter in Boston, the other in Montreal—complete with T-shirts and club stationery.

"He is the face of Calgary," lauds former Calgary Wrangler and Calgary Flame Kelly Kisio. "Even around the whole of Alberta. I doubt you could find anyone—anyone—who has anything to do with sports around this province who doesn't know who Bearcat is."

When Murray was inducted into the Professional Hockey Athletic Trainers Society (PHATS) and Society of Professional Hockey Equipment Managers (SPHEM) back in 2008, Flames retired winger Jim Peplinski summed up the man's jack-of-all-trades persona quite nicely.

"I can't imagine he'll stop here," Calgary's long-time co-captain marvelled. "I'd think this is just the first of many Halls of Fame he'll be inducted into.

"There's the Trainers Hall of Fame.

"The Jockey Hall of Fame.

"The Bus Driving Hall of Fame.

"The Psychologists Hall of Fame.

"The Comedians Hall of Fame

"The Potlickers Hall of Fame.

"He deserves to be in them all. He's one-of-a-kind. A wonderful man, god love him."

One of the finest professional tributes Bearcat can remember came from then-Flames psychologist Hap Day, during just another day down at the rink.

"I honestly thought Hap was sleeping," confesses Bearcat. "Just sitting there in the room. I'm giving Gary Roberts a massage and I'm talkin' to him, like I always talked, telling him how great he was, how he was going to be able to beat this defenceman and how he'd score on the goalie. Getting him ready. Pumping him up. Making him feel good. Just like always. Well, this went on a half hour or so.

"After awhile, Hap got up to leave and I said, 'Geez, Hap, I thought you'd been sleeping!' And he said, 'No, Bear. I haven't been sleeping.

I've been going to school. I've learned more in the last half hour than I did in 10 years at school!'"

Ask any of those entrusted to Bearcat's care and the mention elicits a smile; the emotion is genuine, the regard reciprocal.

"He didn't just look after us," winger Perry Berezan said. "He was there as a sounding board, a psychiatrist, and a cheerleader. If you'll remember, I spent a lot of my brief, undistinguished Flames career in the training room. So I know. Here was someone who didn't have certificates or diplomas. But he knew. He was always reading, studying, making himself better at his job. You felt safe with him. He was a friend. Just a great, great guy.

"Anyone who went through the Flames' dressing room during his time there owes him a debt of gratitude."

Child of the depression, jockey, oil-rig worker, fixer of aches and illnesses, champion of charities, larger-than-life personality, little Jim Murray has enjoyed quite the ride, moving effortlessly from the small-town backstreets and byways of Okotoks, Alberta, to the grand arenas of Madison Square Garden, the Montreal Forum, Maple Leaf Gardens, and the rest.

"Gotta admit," concedes the man himself, chuckling softly. "A helluva story."

So here it is, in his own words.

—G.J.

ONE NIGHT IN MONTREAL...

EVERY MORNING DURING THE STANLEY CUP FINAL SERIES in 1989 against Montreal, I'd be at the arena early and go live on CFAC radio with Jimmy Hughes. I'd give him a fill-in on what was going on.

The day of the second game, before I went on air with Jimmy, Flames head coach Terry Crisp—Crispie—came up to me—he had that look in his eye—and said, "Bearcat, we don't have any injuries and three extra guys. Who would you sit out?"

I just looked at him, kinda confused, and said, "What the hell are you asking me for? I'm just the trainer. You're the coach."

"Well, I'd like to know."

And I finally said, "Well, okay. Nobody. Play 'em all! They're all damn good players!"

And he kinda glared at me and said, "You little sonofabitch…"

So I told him, okay, since you asked me, here are the three I'd sit out. And I gave him the names. Not saying they were bad players or anything—we had such a good team—but he was asking. Later, after warm-up, when the game started, sure enough, all three of those guys I'd picked to sit out were playing.

That told me exactly where I sat with the coach.

Thing is, this happened the next game, the game after that, and the game after that. Same routine, every time: Crispie would ask in the morning, I'd tell him the three guys I'd sit out that night, and all three of those guys would wind up playing.

I was wondering what the hell was going on.

Well, we get to Game 6 and a chance to win the Cup in Montreal. A day I'll never forget. I was on the phone talking with Hughes in the morning as usual and, sure enough, here's Crispie marching down the hallway from the dressing room, right toward me. So I had to tell Jimmy—who's curious about who is and who isn't going to be dressing that night—to hold on a minute.

Lanny, as everyone remembers, hadn't played since the second game of the series.

Crispie came up, again, just about to open his mouth and ask me who I'd sit out, again, and I pointed my finger at him and said, "Crispie, I know what you're going to ask me. What I don't get is why you're going to ask me. You never take my advice. Well, I'll tell you: it doesn't matter who you don't play—you've got to play Lanny. No matter what.

"The team wants him. Everybody wants him. Everybody loves the guy. He's itching. This is his moment. Think of the lift he'd give the guys. You've *got* to play him. I'm done.'"

Crispie gave me a long look, kinda smiled, shook his head at me, and said, "Oh, so now you're coaching..."

And I told him, "Well, maybe it's about time!"

Then off he went.

In Montreal, at the old Forum, if you remember, the dressing rooms were so small. Tiny, tiny. After warm-up, assistant coach Doug Risebrough came into one of these small rooms along with Lanny. I just happened to be in there. Something was up. Riser told me to get out. No way was I leaving, so I moved a few feet and started pretending to fold towels. I looked up and through the door that led into the main dressing room I saw three heads peeking into the room—one was my son and assistant trainer, Allan, as well as Gary Roberts and Joe Nieuwendyk. And Lanny said, "All right, Riser, what's going on? Am I playing or not?"

And Riser told him, "Yeah, you're playing."

I looked at the guys, put my thumb up. All of a sudden, those three heads...gone. Disappeared. *Pffffft!* Like three gophers down a hole. Then, within a few seconds, from the main room, you could hear this roar. Sticks banging on the wall. Guys hollering. The racket was so loud it took Riser, who had his back to me, by surprise.

He turned, saw me, and asked, "Geez, Bear, what's going on?"

I smiled and said, "Don't worry, Riser. Everything's okay.

"We just won the game.

"We just won the Cup."

Riser kinda looked at me, confused. Lanny just winked, then took off. Didn't even stick around to talk to Riser.

And the rest is history...

CHAPTER 2

BEGINNINGS

I LIKE TO SAY I was born into hockey. Literally. From the cradle. The womb. The game was always a part of me.

The nickname Bearcat I inherited from my dad, Allan, a heckuva player in his day. Just a little guy, smaller'n me, and people back then would tell you what a really great skater he was.

I heard all the stories. About how he'd come in on two defencemen and jump between them when they were lining him up, dive down on his belly and slide right through their legs, then up on his skates, and—*pfffft!*—gone.

I used to do the same thing after I started playing.

Could score goals like crazy, my dad.

Well, in those days, they had a team up in Crowsnest Pass, a bunch of Italian coal miners, and it was called the Crowsnest Bearcats. The owner and editor of the *High River Times*, Charles Clark—whose son Joe would go on to be Prime Minister of Canada—liked my dad, liked the way he played, and he started to write stories about him.

Wonderful man, Charlie Clark. Typical newspaper guy. The whole town, the whole area, absolutely loved him.

Years and years later, we played a golf game together one day, in High River, and that night Charlie died. I thought I'd killed him. He had to be in his eighties then.

After we'd finished the golf game, I said, 'Charlie, come in and have a drink and a bite to eat.' And he did. We got to talking—a bunch of us were there by that point—and he ended up having three or four beers. We had a great time. And he was so happy. Then he went home, got into bed and…gone.

I felt terrible. I went and talked to his wife the next day after we'd received the news and she said, "Bear, when he got home he was three feet high in the air. He kept talking about what a great time he had. So don't feel bad."

Anyway, Charlie Clark called my dad the Bearcat in his stories back in the day, because my dad skated and played the way the little Italian guys on the Crowsnest Pass team did. Quick. Skilled. Fearless.

I mean, there actually are bearcats. They look like badgers. They've got one in the Calgary Zoo. And in the Dirty '30s, *bearcat* was also a slang word you heard a lot too. I have no idea what it meant. But you heard it from time to time.

My dad was born in Ontario and the family moved to Killam, where he homesteaded and farmed, when he was five years old.

He was the smallest and second youngest of a family of seven boys and one girl, and quite an athlete. They all were. He played hockey but loved baseball—shortstop was his position—and the baseball team from Granum, the White Sox, drafted him, I guess you'd say, and brought him there.

This was the '20s, remember, and no one had money to pay the players, so the teams found them all jobs. My dad's job was in the grain elevator, and he wound up doing that the rest of his life, eventually winning an award from the Alberta White Pool for longevity as a grain buyer.

Anyway, he was then transferred to Vulcan and the reason was they wanted him over in High River to play hockey in a provincial league, which was almost like playing pro at the time. So they kept moving him closer to High River. In Vulcan he married my mother, Isabelle, and then they moved him to Blackie, which is where I came along.

I was actually born in the Vulcan hospital—my grandparents were living in Vulcan—on January 2, 1933. I was four years old when they moved Dad to Okotoks, and I started playing hockey literally as soon as I could walk.

When we lived in Blackie, across the street from our house—the Alberta Wheat Pool owned it—was a rink. An open-air rink that had these huge, high boards surrounding it, no roof. Out back they had a chute to shovel out the snow. So it was completely enclosed.

My mom would tie up my skates, take me over to the snow pile, let me slide in down the chute and I'd stay there all day. Didn't need a babysitter. I couldn't get out, 'cause it was all boarded up.

That's how I started. We'd skate on the frozen roads, too. Don't know if there were 50 people in the town at the time. So small. It's still small.

My mother was also a very good athlete. A great curler, as well as being a pretty good skater and a basketball player in Vulcan. In fact, in basketball, before even meeting my dad, she was picked for a team from southern Alberta that would practice with and play games against the Edmonton Grads, one of the most famous teams in Canadian basketball history, who won the first women's world championship! And my mom was one of five girls picked to get the Grads ready for the big tournaments.

She was that good.

She was a fine tennis player too, and later, when were in Okotoks, she was always on the ladies' curling team, as my dad was on the men's.

She grew up in Vulcan, with five sisters and a brother. My dad moved there, they met, and they got married.

About the only time I ever heard her complain was back here in Okotoks when Dad would walk into the house with some guy, never telling her he was bringing anybody, to be fed. Almost always, he really needed feeding, so she'd grumble a little bit but they'd wind up getting a meal. Had a big heart, my mom. Everybody in the community here loved her.

I'm very proud of both of them.

Everything was so different back then, of course. You could just walk into the houses of your friends without even knocking. "Oh, there's little Jimmy Murray!"

Welcomed, all the time. It was, in that sense, a wonderful way to grow up.

The other nickname that's stuck with me, "Potlicker," my dad gave me because I'd lick the pot as clean as a whistle after Mom would make a cake. My sister, Annabelle, two years younger than me, always ended up with the icing dish because she was the smallest. So I'd get the cake mix.

Working at the grain elevator, my dad was well-known around the town and the area, of course, and so when he started calling me Little Potlicker, everyone else did, too.

I always tell everybody it's better than being called Little Sonofabitch.

Growing up at that time, during the depression—the Dirty '30s—I'm sure is why I got involved with all the charities I've worked with through-out the years—and continue to work with. The idea of helping people started back then. Because that's what people did.

My best friend for a while in Blackie—we shot gophers together—and his family lived above a garage. I would have been around four years old at the time. I went up one day to visit him and his family, and they were having dinner. I was sitting there and his mom asked me if I wanted anything to eat. I said, "No, thanks. I'm fine."

I was watching, kinda confused, and I asked, "Why are you eating porridge for dinner?" I didn't really get an answer so when I got home I asked my dad what that was all about. He explained to me that my friend's family didn't have any money and the only thing they had to eat was boiled wheat—wheat that he'd given them. All the grain elevator guys and a lot of the farmers did that—gave people wheat to help out, did what they could.

I can remember that as if it was yesterday. Being in that room over the garage. Asking that question. Not understanding. It left such an impression. It just hit me. *Wham*! Some people didn't have enough to eat. I'd really never thought of it in those terms before. I mean, considering the times, we were doing better than most families.

Those were lean days for pret' near everybody. We lived about a block and a half from the elevator where my dad worked—there must've been six or seven of those elevators in a row. And the train, which ran right by there, would be full of guys riding the boxcars. All of them were from Ontario—doctors, lawyers, business guys, you name it—and they came out west because they could always get work here, on the farms, whether it was harvest or not.

They'd jump out of the boxcars and my dad would be at the train stop there to meet 'em and tell 'em, "See that yellow house down there? Go to the back door and my wife'll feed you." Well, I was a little kid and I'd be out there on the back step talking to these guys. Curious, you know. They turned out to be the most interesting people. So friendly. So well-spoken. So intelligent. And here they were riding in boxcars a long way from home, looking for any kind of work.

Those are things you don't forget easily.

Then World War II came along. I still remember at that time I was just starting to play hockey and my dad was coaching. All these older guys—18, 19, 20 years old—playing in Okotoks, local guys, were my heroes. I idolized them. Most of them played for kind of a junior team my dad had started, the Okotoks Drillers. I still have one of those jerseys in the house.

All of a sudden, they were gone! Off to war. My heroes. The only people left in town were kids like me or older adults. Everything changed, for a while. I remember once time I walked past the pub out near the old ball diamond—my dad played a lot of baseball—and no one was there. Just deserted. The noise—I can still hear it—of the wind going through the chicken wire backstop. An eerie noise. And I remember walking around that diamond and finding an old baseball, with half the hide cover torn off, down the first-base line. Funny how things like that noise and that baseball, because of the time we were living through then, stick with you.

We had those ration books during those years. You couldn't get food without 'em. Sugar, flour, salt, all those kinds of things. My mother would tear this large stamp out of a ration book and I'd take it down to the grocery store and trade it for a pound of sugar. Well, the mothers in town started swapping these stamps—not food, the stamps—for what they needed more of.

I spent some time as a jockey. When I was about 10 or 11, my dad bought a horse from a rodeo guy in Black Diamond, a famous cowboy named Thompson. My dad dealt with all those guys, bought their grain. So he purchased this old mare, a roping horse. Well, I got pretty excited. Bingo, I was on that horse like a shot. An Appaloosa. The horse was pregnant. It had been bred to a Stampede rodeo champion roper from Okotoks and I'd gone to school with the guy's kids.

The horse gave birth and the foal was mine from the day it was born. I grew up riding this horse, bareback. I loved riding it. Like everybody at one time owned a bike to ride, back then I had this horse. I'd go down to the river and fish off the horse's back. Those were my play-grounds—the mountains, the streams, and the rivers. I also used to do a lot of tricks on the horse, same way I did on the ice—laying overtop of it like a sack, on my back with my feet in the air, riding standing up. Having a great time.

I would be practicing these tricks on the road outside the elevator where my dad worked. And one day this guy saw me while he was vis-iting the elevator buying grain. Turned out he was a racehorse man who owned the champion horse for the Western Racing Circuit. He asked my dad, "Think he'd like to be a jockey?" (I was just a little guy.) My dad said, "Why don't you ask him yourself?" So he came out and asked me. And I said, "Would I?! You betcha!"

Among my heroes in those days were those great jockeys—Johnny Longden, Eddie Arcaro, Willie Shoemaker. So he took me out and signed me to a contract. I was 13. I moved out to his farm on May 24, helping him harvest, doing the farm work, exercising the horses. That's how I got started, even though I never actually raced for him because he was hiring all these hotshot jockeys. So eventually I got p—ed off and quit because I wasn't getting to ride. I said to hell with it, cancelled the contract.

My best friend in Okotoks was Norm Haynes, the toughest SOB this side of the valley. He played hockey, kicked the crap out of everybody. Norm Haynes' father was like a second father to me. Norm was a good, intermediate-type hockey player and my first friend. He wasn't mean, but he was tough in a *don't p—s him off* way. As I said, his dad, Bill, was my mentor. Geez, he was a wonderful man. Like a second father. I'd walk a mile and half up to their place. Bill didn't fool around, but he taught me so many things. They had a fold-out bed and three of us would sleep in it. I remember him telling me, "Get up! Get up!" But I wouldn't. I was sleeping, or at least pretending that I didn't hear him. Well, he just folded the bed up against the wall, with me in it, upside down! Old Bill, he taught me how to be a growing boy, how to behave, stay out of trouble, do things right.

Norm went on to become the head chuckwagon man for many, many years. So I started hanging with him and I started riding on my own, every weekend. Medicine Hat. Gleichen. High River. My very first race, I remember, was in Millarville on a grass track. I did that until I was 18. Then I got too heavy. I weighed 118 pounds, and I couldn't hold my job. Couldn't ride anymore.

SHIRLEY MURRAY
Bearcat's wife

Jim and I met in Estevan, Saskatchewan. A girlfriend of mine, Lois, her folks had places selling hamburgers and french fries, both at the rink and down by the river. And this guy would always come around. My girlfriend would always be saying, "Look up there." And there'd be Jimmy, down by the river, sitting in a car, watching me. I'd work at a dance and wouldn't you know it, he'd be there. Just couldn't get rid of him.

One time, Lois' dad goes outside, grabs Jim, and says, "If you're gonna sit out here all day, you're coming in here to peel potatoes." So he hauled him in and Jim peeled potatoes, sitting on a five-gallon pail, upside down, every day. The people I worked for would always give me a hard time, telling me, "Oh, he's *such* a nice guy, Shirley! Be nice to him!" Then they'd have him over when I was there and I'd get so mad. I'm afraid I was really mean to him.

Initially, I liked the guy. Then he seemed to be around all the time and I didn't like him so much. I'd be at the rink, where Lois was selling coffee and ice cream, and Jimmy'd be playing. And he'd be fighting. All the time. None of the other hockey players seemed to be fighting. But the little guy always was. I thought he was going to get himself killed.

But he was persistent. And eventually he won me over. We'd go dancing—loved dancing. Jim's a very good dancer. Other people used to stop on the dance floor and watch us. We just loved jiving. After we got married, we moved five times—in Estevan alone. I'd only moved once, then I got married and moved five times. That was the oil boom.

Jim was away a lot, first on the oil rigs and then after he became a trainer. When I was alone with no kids I kinda felt sorry for myself. But after Allan and then Danny came along, you just get used to it. That's your life.

I finally got used to hockey and we had three young guys living with us. Jimmy Watson was one of them. He'd go on to play with Philadelphia, with his brother, Joe, and he loved that team even when he was younger and Joe was already there.

We had one guy live with us, Darel Oakford—he got so attached to us and us to him that when he left, he wouldn't even come home to pack his bags. I cried and got so mad at the coach, Cec Papke, that I refused to talk to him for a while. Very quiet kid, Oakie. He'd sit and we'd talk after breakfast and the other two would be like, "Hey, we've got to get to practice!" The one thing I found out quick was that hockey players do like to eat. They eat all the time. But they were all good guys. We had a lot of traffic in the house for awhile: the three hockey players, our two boys, and I babysat four other kids. I don't know where we put 'em all, to be honest. We only had two bedrooms in the house. So they all slept downstairs. I washed all their clothes. We had clotheslines out back in the yard and all the neighbours would ask me, "*What* on earth are you doing, Shirley?!"

Then in the summer, when hockey school was on, we had those guys around too. So it was always pretty busy around our house. But that was fine. That was our life. The night we won the Cup in Montreal, well, it was wonderful. I knew how much it meant to Jim. To everybody. I got to go to a lot of great events and meet a lot of nice people. I had the chance to drink out of the Cup. I remember Ardell McDonald, Lanny's wife, she's pulling me along, saying, "We're going on the ice! We're going to party!" She was sitting with me, was always so good to me, taking care of me. Whenever there was a bus to catch, she'd be like, "Shirley! Come on!" She treated me like a sister.

All the wives were wonderful, the players and the owners. Once a month they'd arrange a get-together, a lunch, and invite Bobby's wife and me. The Flames were a real family. The wives, the girlfriends, everyone was included. We had a ball. Before then, the women weren't invited to a lot of things on a lot of clubs. But our club was so good. We were never left out. That was Cliff. And Harley. We'd visit their homes for get-togethers, go on some trips, everything was taken care of.

I felt included, involved, a part of everything. That was special. We were very lucky.

CHAPTER 3

THE COWBOY WAY

I WASN'T A COWBOY, but I've always been a cowboy's friend. Put it that way.

I grew up on horseback. Okotoks was, is, my home, but Turner Valley/Black Diamond was No. 2. I rode racehorses and chuckwagon horses, in flat races. Not wagon races. I'd go out to Black Diamond—all my buddies are still out there, most of them 6'6" and meaner'n a junkyard dog. Wilf Girletz, the famous bull rider, was one.

I dealt with these guys all the time. Me, just a little 112-pound SOB jockey. But they treated me like I was King Tut from Turd Island. Simply great people.

Norm Haynes, when he got older, as I mentioned, rode chuckwagons. Every race, every summer, every night. After I'd gotten too heavy to jockey, Norm said, "Come ride for us." Every little town, every day—High River, Fort McLeod, Nanton, down in Montana—I'd ride on weekends.

During the Calgary Stampede, we'd live there on the grounds in this big roundhouse at one end of the old Victoria Arena, right where the Saddledome is today. Inside there were stalls, all around, and in the middle we would have a bonfire going. After the races everybody—the guys exercising the horses, like me; the outriders; and the riders—would come in to drink and talk. Had a helluva time.

Well, who became one of our favourite people? The bull-fighter—rodeo clown, I guess you'd call him today. It was Slim Pickens! The guy who rode the bomb in that movie *Dr. Strangelove or: How I Learned to Stop Worrying and Love the Bomb.* He went on and acted in a whole bunch of cowboy movies too. But back then, he worked as a bullfighter and he'd get in that roundhouse at the end of Victoria Arena, tell jokes, bull— with everybody, and he was, let me tell you, hilarious. He came up with different tricks to do with the bulls during the rodeo too. You thought he was nuts on TV? You should've seen him live. I was 17 and my mouth was wide open, dropped clear down to the ground, having a few beers and watching this guy perform. What a hoot!

Norm and I always hung around together in those days. The guy that brought him in there and hired him was the Stampede chuckwagon champion for 10 to 12 years.

My job was to look after the horses. Norm ran in 10 races on a night and his brother rode in another eight. I had 18 horses to look after! Plus the one I was riding made 19. When the cowboys were riding in through the infield they'd come into the chute, give me the reins of the horse they'd just ridden, and grab the reins of another horse.

When it was all over, I was in charge of 18 tired horses. Between races, I had to exercise the horses. I've gotta tell you this story, 'cause it became famous around the chuckwagon circuit. One time, we're halfway through a night and this big palooka, huge SOB, wearing a purple hat with a small brim—I'll never forget that, real crappy hat—comes in yelling, "I need a horse! I need a horse!" And I'm going, "Well, you can't have any of these horses!" I'm on a horse, looking after eight other horses, and he just grabbed one of ours. Took the reins right out of my hands! Norm came in a bit later and said, "Where's my horse?" I told him this guy in a purple hat with a small brim took it. Well, Norm's madder'n hell, but what was I gonna do? I'm a 112-pound scrawny little runt on top of a horse looking after all these other horses and this big SOB comes in and takes one.

Norm calmed down, but he had to race one race with a horse who had already run. He wasn't very happy about that. Thankfully, we ended up winning. We're in the barn afterward, sitting around, and guess who strolls in the back door? The guy in the purple hat. So I find Norm and tell him, "Hey, the guy in the purple hat's over there."

He says, "Thanks, Bear."

And next thing you know Norm is kicking the living hell out of this guy. I mean, laying a beating on him. Damn near killed the guy.

The lesson in all this: never mess with Norm.

Those cowboys, they accepted me and treated me so well. One time, the Stampede Board was fighting with the Cowboys Association and ended up cancelling Rodeo Royal and the Stampede. In essence, they fired the cowboys. So the cowboys went to this World Association, divided themselves up into four, and called it Team Rodeo.

This is when Alec Recsky—my mentor-in-training—and I got together and started talking about travelling around looking after the cowboys, taping 'em up and all that. We had sponsors like Justin Boots coming out the ying-yang, but Alec, because of his job with the Calgary Stampeders, couldn't do the two, so I ended up doing it all. Eventually we both backed out and three or four guys, paramedics, took over.

But those cowboys, let me tell you, are the toughest SOBs going. Because they have to ride to get paid. If you're playing hockey and have a bruised shin, you don't have to play because you're gonna be too slow. But you still get your cheque. These guys have got to compete to get any money and then do well to make good money. I've seen guys go out and do their thing despite broken legs. So you'd get a tremendous amount of experience handling certain injuries the cowboys were always dealing with. Like shoulders for the bull riders. Geez, I'd be taping some of those guys up like they were mummies! Just so they could ride.

And I had more of those guys come back and say, "Bear, if I hadn't had you here I never woulda made that final and cashed that cheque." Made you feel good.

But we—Alec Recsky and I—really went to school on it and learned a lot. I got two years out of that and then they got things sorted out and went back to regular rodeo. To this day, I'm still in touch with some of those guys.

Cowboys…can't say anything except they're wonderful, wonderful people.

CHAPTER 4

GETTING INTO
THE BUSINESS

MY VERY FIRST JOB as a trainer was with the junior Centennials after I transferred back to Calgary from Estevan in June of '63. I was very excited to be moving back home. I started playing for the Okotoks Oilers in the Big Six, which was senior Allan Cup hockey. At that time, Shirley and I were expecting our son Danny to be born any day. So I got to Calgary and the company I was working for by then—an outfit called Import Tool, where I was a field/sales representative—kept asking how far along Shirley was, when she was due, that kind of stuff.

One day I came into the office and the first question, like every day, was, "That kid born yet?" And I told 'em, proud as all get-out, "About two hours ago. A boy. Everybody's doing great."

And then they said, well, that's great, oh, and by the way, we're moving you back to Estevan. In a month, month and a half.

What?

They explained to me that the customers back there were madder'n hell, they liked me a lot, and they were ticked off that I'd moved out of there.

Well, I got upset. I told them, "You might be sending me back to Estevan, but I'm not going. What I am doing is going out the door over there and it's not going to hit me on the a— on the way out." So I walked away from a very, very good job.

27

It had been so busy in Estevan that these guys I knew from the job had formed their own companies and had done very well for themselves. Well, one guy came to me and asked whether I'd like to represent him and his business in Calgary to keep making contacts for them. So I wound up starting a company and did that for a bunch of those guys, 10 or 12 of them, and did very well working for them.

At this time, my buddy back in Estevan, Cec Papke, came to me and told me he and two other guys had bought the junior hockey team and were forming this league called the Western Canadian Major Junior league—which is now the Western Hockey League, of course—to compete with the Eastern leagues in Ontario and Quebec. There were a bunch of guys involved in the league—Scotty Munro, Bill Hunter, Benny Hatskin from Winnipeg.

And Cec told me, "Bear, we need a trainer. I could sure use you." I thought about it; I had some friends who were already trainers around town I talked to pretty regularly. I was interested. So after considering the offer, I finally told Cec that I'd love to do it. It was a big change for me, and I was leaving a good thing. But Shirley was on board. That meant everything, sealed the deal. And, as I said, I loved hockey. So, okay, let's go.

I started out as a jack of all trades. I'd go and tack up posters advertising the games near the motels along MacLeod Trail to generate some publicity—Hockey Game Tonight! Plus, I'd sharpen skates, in addition to doing PR and all this other stuff.

I worked my a— off. But I loved it. I even scouted players! I scouted Cec's first two guys, as a matter of fact. One of them, Ervie Miller, was playing for Okotoks; the other, Brian Carlin, was playing for Gleichen. They were playing in the midget playoffs against each other. I told him, "Cec, you gotta come out and see these guys." He took one look at 'em and signed 'em that night.

Carlin suffered maybe the worst injury I ever saw. I had a few others that were really bad. Al MacInnis suffered a dislocated hip one time that was really bad. A lot more serious than we thought. One of those things where he got taken into the boards behind the net. We got him onto a stretcher quick and off to the hospital. Later, we were told his hip had been dislocated *forward*. A very serious injury, but he came through it well. We were lucky. And Gary Roberts had that awful quadricep hematoma injury the one time. But Carlin's…I still remember it. He got hit in front of our net and was obviously in trouble. I jumped out onto the ice. He was lying on his stomach and his one foot had broken and twisted and was actually pointing the wrong way, up into the air. The opposite of what it should've been. Awful. I took one look and said to myself, *Oh, god….* Everything was torn, a spiral fracture of the lower leg bones. But he recovered and played again.

There were so many good guys on that team. Rusty Patenaude from B.C., a farm kid. Tough, small. I liked him a lot. Mike Rogers. We've been friends for such a long time.

MIKE ROGERS
Calgary Centennials, 1971–74

In juniors, Centennials owner and coach Scotty Munro was too cheap to get us a new bus. This was an old bus. On this bus, nothing worked. Certainly not the front-window defrost. So there would be Bearcat, during snowstorms, scraping ice off the window with a credit card, his head out the side window and manning the wheel with his right hand.

Scotty also used to buy sticks and they all arrived straight. As soon as we saw the sticks, Danny Gare, Jerry Holland, and myself would take our sticks and head off to one of the washrooms in the Corral, turn on the hot water, and curve 'em. Scotty was dead-set against that because, god, if you broke a stick and it cost him money, he'd kill you. Well, he found out about the three of us, what we were doing, and sent Bearcat to hunt us down. We'd go into these washrooms and Bearcat would always find us. So we finally found one washroom, way at the back of the Corral, other side from the dressing room. We thought, *He's not going to waste his time coming all the way over there.* But we decided to have a spotter, anyway—two of us would be curving the sticks and the other guy would be peeking through the bathroom door, as a lookout. Well, sure enough, there's Bearcat, going to every bathroom, one by one. We figure he's got to get bored and quit but, being Bearcat, of course he doesn't and soon he's marching toward the bathroom we're in.

So whatta we do, whatta we do? Well, the three of us go into the stalls, close the doors, lock 'em, stand on the toilet seats, and go totally quiet. We figure Bear's going to come in, take a quick look, see we're not there, and leave. We hear the door open and close. Good. He's gone. Then all of a sudden, down below us, underneath the doors, here's this little bald head peeking through.

And all he said was, "Gotcha!"

Bob Nystrom was with us for a couple years, too. Scotty helped him a lot. He was one of the group we got from the B.C. provincial league team in Kamloops Scotty bought and used as our farm team. Then Bobby was drafted by the Islanders, went there and won all those Cups, scored the big goals everyone remembers. They had a bunch of Western kids on that team on Long Island—Clark Gillies, Bryan Trottier, Butch Goring, Brent Sutter—so he fit right in.

When he was here, just a young guy, Bobby was very popular with everybody, including the girls. He had his hands full there. A big, good-looking guy, charismatic, but he handled it pretty well for someone his age.

And, of course, we had Danny Gare.

Danny and I hit it off immediately. He was such a tough little s—t. You didn't fool with him. He wasn't a big kid but he stood up to everybody. I could relate to that, of course, being a little guy myself. Not as tough, but we definitely had the size part in common.

So I respected him more than a lot of people did at the time, I guess. It didn't surprise me at all when Danny went on to have such a darned good NHL career in Buffalo. Other people, maybe. Not me. I still follow him on Facebook and I love listening to him and seeing what he's up to. Knowing that I know him and that we're friends gives me a good feeling in my heart.

In those days, the scouts who came to practices would come and grab me for information. I was, after all, on the inside. They'd ask things like, "How does this guy get along with his landlady? How does he get along with his girlfriend? How does he get along with other people? How's he doing in school?" All these kinds of questions. I should've been charging them for all the information I was giving out!

They knew I was in the know because I'd always be talking to the landladies, making sure the guys ate properly, got their sleep, weren't horsing around. If there was any kind of problem, I told the landladies to call me. Not the coach or anyone else. Me. I'd take care of things. But I have to say, the guys—and they were young kids, remember—were pretty good about everything. I can't remember having any real serious issues.

Anyway, in the dressing room, I'd use Danny as my helper. My sergeant major, I called him. I'd go to him when I had trouble with another player—the guy was being ornery, maybe—and say, "Danny, so-and-so needs to be taken outside," rather than go to the guy myself and disrupt things.

They could get pretty cocky, these kids. I had trouble in that sense at times. I remember one guy, Geoff Wilson—Carey Wilson's brother. This was when I was working with the Wranglers. He was a wise-a—, big-shot doctor's son. Complete opposite of Carey, who would play for the Flames and was a wonderful, wonderful guy.

First practice, Geoff came in, took his stuff off, threw it on the floor, showered, and left. I said to the coach, Doug Sauter, "You gotta straighten this guy out." Doug said, "Bear, that's your job." Okay. So I left the equipment right where it was. Didn't hang it up. Nothing. Anyway, Wilson came into the room the next day and it was still lying there.

Doug told him, "Wear it." So he stormed in after practice that day, mad at me, and did the very same thing. Just tossed his stuff on the floor. So I waited until he was gone, gathered up the equipment, threw it in the shower, and turned on the water. I let it soak awhile and left it there. Well, he came in the next day and it was still there, soaking wet and laying in the shower.

He said, "Where's my equipment?" I said, "I don't know. What did *you* do with it?"

Well, eventually he found it in the shower. After that, I didn't have a problem with him throwing his stuff on the floor anymore.

My whole career, I didn't want to coach or manage or anything like that. I just wanted the players to have respect for me, for everybody else—Bobby Stewart and Allan with the Flames, because those guys worked their butts off—and have respect for their equipment.

Anyway, Danny Gare took care of those things for me with the Centennials. He didn't throw anybody's equipment in the shower, of course. He'd just have them off in a corner, up against a wall. Those guys would be far more willing to listen to Danny—everybody respected and listened to Danny—than to me. So that's why I'd go and seek his help. And Danny would call over the guy who was being difficult and straighten him out. Immediately. Then he'd come back and say, "Bear, it's done." That's all. "It's done." No fuss. No drama. And no problems after that.

Those were interesting times. That Cec, he was a crazy bastard. He wanted to sign this one kid, but the kid had already signed a player card for another team, was playing for them, and had been suspended. That didn't matter to Cec. He just said, "That's okay. We'll just change his name." So suddenly this kid became Zipchuk. That's the last name Cec gave him—Zipchuk. And he signed another player card, for us. Well, the league found out and suspended Cec. During the time Cec was suspended, I ended up running the practices. I even coached one game, against the Edmonton Oil Kings. And we won! So I like to say I'm 1–0 as a coach, and a fan actually wrote a really nice poem about me coaching that game.

Shoot, I wasn't even really a trainer yet and already I was coaching?

Then Scotty Munro took over. He already had the team in Estevan but he could see that the franchise in Calgary was by far the better money-maker. So he left Estevan, because the league rules were that he couldn't have two teams, came to Calgary, and within two days he had fired Cec. Cec then moved over to the Calgary Canucks. I decided to stay with the Centennials.

JOHN DAVIDSON
Calgary Centennials, 1969–70, 1971–73; former New York Rangers president

I've got boxes and boxes and boxes of stuff. And with everything on hold during Covid-19, I was sorting through the stuff, and believe me; there's a lot about Bearcat Murray and the Centennials in there. And the memories it jogged...

I'm 67 years old now. I was in my late teens then. Basically everything for me started there, then, with the Centennials organization, Bearcat Murray along with Scotty Munro and his family. Everything that's happened to me... it's been an amazing ride.

When I was a broadcaster in New York, I'd be sitting in Madison Square Garden at 4:30 in the afternoon in the booth, with nobody there, and think, *Geezus, I'm just a kid from Calgary. What in hell am I doing here?! How in hell did that happen?!*

And then I was sitting here thinking, *I'm president of the New York Rangers. How in hell did that happen?!*

Well, you trace it backward and it all started in Calgary, with the Centennials, and one of the people at the forefront—without question—is

Bearcat Murray. I have nothing but fantastic memories of the man. Imagine the thousands and thousands of people he's worked with, he's helped, over the years. I kinda came out of nowhere and ended up with the Centennials. Scotty sent Marty Kissel and myself, as kids, to High Prairie, Alberta, to play in a senior men's league. And then I ended up coming back to the Centennials halfway through the season and played behind Eddie Dyck. I got in for three minutes the rest of the year. Bearcat and Scotty were running the show.

I went to Lethbridge for a year, with Lanny McDonald, and then the following two years I came back to Calgary. We were the only thing going in town in the wintertime then. We filled the Corral. We were the talk of the town for sports.

And Bearcat was at the front of it all. He did everything. Looked after us. Drove the bus. Fixed the bus. One night we played in Edmonton, stayed at the MacDonald Hotel, which was pretty nice for us, and drove the next morning to Saskatoon to play the next night. An ice storm. Every, oh, 20 minutes, Bearcat, the driver, had to stop, get out, and scrape the ice off the windshield and the wipers. Then we'd go another 20 minutes. Stop. Another 20. Stop. And on and on. All. Day. Long.

Well, we got there at 7 o'clock at night, got our stuff, and ended up playing at 9:30 or 10, and the place is full. And who's taking care of the players? Bearcat Murray. The guy driving the bus and stopping every 20 minutes to get rid of the ice. It was incredible. Reminds me of Ed Sheeran or one of those musicians who can get nine different things going, then play the guitar and it sounds like a band playing.

When we were in the Corral the bench wasn't very wide but it was three rows deep. Almost tiered. And the boards seemed like they were six feet high. We were kids playing a man's game. That was *man's* hockey at the time, let me tell you. And when Bearcat had to jump over the boards because someone got hurt, it was like a game of leapfrog. Such a high-energy person. No dust on him at all.

I was from Calgary but a lot of the other guys weren't. And Bearcat took care of a lot of us for a very long time. That's very special. There's probably not a person in hockey that I have more respect for than Bearcat Murray.

Starting on the training side of it, I understood that I had a lot to learn. What I found out very quickly, though, was that I knew a lot more than I thought I did because of my years as a jockey, working with the horse trainers, exercising the horses, tending to the horses' injuries.

I'm self-taught. I always read up on what was new about injuries and health and such. Anything I could get my hands on. One of the best friends I ever had was Alec Recsky, who I mentioned before. He was the athletic guy for the downtown YMCA in Calgary. He ran programs and all that. I got to know him when I was working with the Centennials and he was a great teacher. He then became the head trainer for the CFL Stampeders football team and brought me in to help during the summer for training camp and the home games. Being with him for those five years, I learned so much. Vince Murphy was in charge of the medical staff with the Stamps and he was so generous with his time, too.

My son Allan had been working with us with the Centennials and he came out to McMahon Stadium with me to continue his education as a therapist.

ALLAN MURRAY
Assistant trainer, Calgary Centennials, Calgary Cowboys,
Calgary Wranglers, Calgary Flames; Bearcat's son
I got started with Dad at 12 years old as a stick boy for the Centennials. I just enjoyed being part of a team, the enthusiasm that went with it. And, of course, I enjoyed working beside my dad.

I remember watching NHL games with him at our little house in Altadore and going to Big Six games at the Corral. Then, one night years later, you find yourself at the Forum in Montreal and the clock's ticking down and you know you're going to be part of a team that wins the Stanley Cup, and you're sharing that moment with your dad? Unbelievable.

Who'd have ever thought it'd be possible? Not me. Not in a million years. And to have Grandpa there, too.... Grandpa would come to every home game at the 'Dome, drive in from Okotoks, then catch the CTrain to the rink. After the game I'd give him a ride back to his car so he could get back to Okotoks. He was the reason Dad got into hockey, loved it so much. Then Dad passed that on to me. So to have him there, when we got to celebrate in Montreal, was amazing. And his name's kinda on the Cup, too, because I was named after him. That's pretty neat.

As far as the players were concerned, Dad was just so...reliable. They could call him at three in the morning if they were having any kind of trouble. If they had trouble with their kids being sick they could call him, too. No one ever worried about Bearcat not coming through. He was always there.

Jack Gotta was the coach of the Stampeders then. I loved Jocko. John Hufnagel was the quarterback at that time and his favourite receiver was Tommy Forzani. Wonderful, wonderful guys.

I remember one time Alec had been continually bugging me to teach him about fly fishing. Well, the day after every game, Jocko would have a practice with shorts and helmets only. We were down on the grass on the south side of the stadium. I figured we weren't doing anything important, so that'd be the best time to show Alec how to fly fish. I brought my rods down there and the players were just kind of goofing off, and I started casting, not paying any attention to what was going on on the field. All of a sudden I got a tap on my shoulder. I turned around and it's Gotta standing there—tall guy, hands on hips—and he

36

asked me what the hell was going on. I told him, "Alec wants to learn how to fly fish."

He looked at me, smiled, and said, "You know what, Bearcat? I appreciate you trying to help old Alec but I'm trying to run a practice here. Do you mind?"

All the players had stopped what they were doing and they were all standing there, watching me fly fish! Oh, geez. I thought I was in real trouble—maybe I'd gone too far—but Jocko laughed and laughed. Like I said, good guy.

The very same thing happened once with Scotty Bowman in Detroit. Not fly fishing, but talking. Mikey Vernon was there by then. Well, the Red Wings were coming out for practice in the morning before us. We saw Mikey and he came over to talk, of course. I guess we kinda lost track of time. Scotty skated over and leaned on the boards.

"Hey, Bear, how things going?"

"Fine, Scotty, fine. You?"

"Not bad. Can't complain. Except that I can't get practice started because I'm missing one of my goaltenders. And he's a pretty important guy."

Scotty, by the way, is the one who started the whole "Bearcat's the only goalie in history to be plus-1" thing after the Flames scored that playoff goal against L.A. while I was on the ice looking after Vernon. Scotty was doing colour commentary on TV at the time, and on the air he told everyone that I was officially plus-1. And it's the truth, I guess.

Anyway, back to the Stampeders. We had a lot of great people back then. Terry Irvin, a defensive back. I got along good with him. Doug Battershill, who played linebacker and went on to become a chiropractor, was another one. Willie Armstead is a guy I loved. And oh, Woz—defensive end Lyall Woznesensky—was a nut.

During one of those day-after-game practices they were all out there horsing around. Woz was at the far end, fielding kicks. All of a sudden he was running toward the ball yelling, "I got it! I got it!" Well, he got it all right. Right through his hands—*pow!*—and right in the nuts. Went down as if he'd been shot and lay on the field, moaning. Everyone was killing themselves laughing.

Sometimes things got a little strange. I'd learned this one trick from Cec Papke way back, a fun thing. A player'd be reading the paper and I'd come along and kick it out of his hands. Then I'd grab it while it was still the air and just keep walking—and now *I'd* be reading the paper.

We'd just signed or traded for this kid from Winnipeg, a good ball-player, and I couldn't figure out why the Bombers would let him go. So I did this thing with the paper, kicking it out of his hands, just fiddling around. Then Alec went up to the guy and he said, joking-like, "You've got to be careful with Bearcat. He's pretty quick and he sure can run." And the guy just looked at Alec and replied, "If he's that fast, can he outrun a bullet?"

Alec said to me, "Bear, I think you'd better keep your eye on that guy."

Alec formed a club for all the trainers in the area and we'd head out to schools and do demos, taping and things of that nature. While I was doing that, I slid over for a couple of those years to help out Russ Parker and the baseball team as business manager, doing programs, whatever was needed. The ballpark was right next door to the football stadium so everything was really close, and everything worked out real good.

Initially with the Centennials we travelled to away games in these damn station wagons. And the players would drive them. Well, we'd be going to someplace like Prince Albert in the dead of winter, a snowstorm would hit full-blast, and they'd get lost. We never had an issue or someone being late or missing a game, but there was always that possibility. Drove Scotty nuts.

So after awhile he told me, "Bear, we need to get a bus. I can't put up with this s—t anymore." I had a friend whose brother was the head mechanic for Greyhound in Calgary. I went and talked to him and together we drove up to Edmonton, picked out a bus, and away we went.

Naturally, I drove the bus. But that was crazy too. We'd be on the highway and—this sounds terrible now—the guys would have me trying to run down gophers. The kids would be at the front of the bus, pointing and yelling, "There's one over there, Bear!"

Well, we did a pretty good job of clearing the gophers out of Saskatchewan.

CHAPTER 5

THE PROFESSIONAL RANKS

I TURNED PRO when the Cowboys of the World Hockey Association came to town. I was the trainer there for two years, then the owner, Jim Pattison, just shut it down, walked away. Only two years, as I mentioned, but they were sure fun. Different. They were all crazy, those guys. A great baptism into the pro game for me.

Scotty Munro had wanted to be a part of the WHA initially, but he didn't trust the guy running it, so he backed out. Before the Cowboys arrived he actually had a WHA team all set to go called the Broncs. The logo was a horse's head. Everything seemed to be good to go, then the owner got sick and Scotty pulled the pin, took a disliking to the guy running the league, and said, "No bloody way I'm getting involved and putting my money in!" There we were, just sitting there, and the team went to Cleveland.

Anyway, three years later, the Cowboys finally came to town. The sad thing is that Scotty was going to be involved, but he died of cancer in late September 1975. I was supposed to take a jersey of the team to show him up to the hospital, the Calgary General in Little Italy, but he never got to see it. That saddens me to this day.

Harry Howell, a Hall of Famer, was one of our assistant captains and helped coach too. A wonderful man. A really good friend of Joe Crozier's, our head coach at the time. Crozier...I was scared to death of him at first, had heard all the stories about how tough he was. He had a reputation as a real disciplinarian. And the reputation was apparently well-earned. He'd get madder'n a SOB. I remember one game we'd played really bad. Next day we're at the Corral for practice and he came over and told me, giving me a heads-up, "Bearcat, *no* water on the bench today. No *nothing*. We're going to have a really tough practice, most of it skating. This is a discipline thing I do. I don't want any tomfoolery from these players."

So he started skating 'em. And skating 'em. Forward, backward, figure eights. One way, then back the other. Well, after awhile the guys were hurting, and they started yelling, "Bear! Bear! Water! Water!" Well, all I could do was shrug, like, *Yeah. Sorry. I'm trying!*

Though all of this, Joe just stood at centre ice with the butt end of his stick tucked under his chin, blade on the ice. Leaning on the stick, not moving, just watching. He'd brought this coffee cup out with him, for effect, I guess. And every once in awhile he'd hold that cup in the air—meaning more coffee. So I'd run out and fill up it up.

Meanwhile, the guys were dying. So one time I got out there with a refill and I just had to tell him, "Joe, I don't mean to overstep my bounds or anything. You're the coach. But I'm a little concerned about what's happening and that you're opening yourself up to a possible mutiny here, or maybe even a lawsuit. Because you cannot keep the players from having water. That's a no-no. They're liable to turn around and sue ya. Which would be a disaster."

He thought about that for a little while, leaned harder on that stick of his, and finally grunted. "Huh! Okay. Put the water on the bench."

Well, on my way off the ice I threw my arms in the air like a championship boxer that'd just won a fight and the guys started cheering. I honestly thought I might get fired. But Joe and I, from that day on, were the best of friends. He treated me so good after that. I could not believe the change in him. He was old-school. The oldest. But I was used to that after the coaches I'd been through—Scotty Munro, Cec Papke, that gang. Rough and tough, Joe. But he was alone running that team. Poor old Scotty had died, leaving Joe with the two jobs.

Joe's wife, Bonnie, was a character. The reason she liked me was because I had the same name as their racehorse, Teddybearcat. Yup, that was the horse's actual name. One time, Joe and Bonnie rented a trailer—not a motor home, a trailer—and set it up down by the Bow River at Shangri-La, my favourite summer getaway place. Well, she had to shower three times a day. *Had* to, for whatever reason. You got down there and there was no water to wash with. It's a river. Well, they ran out of water right away! We had to haul water in by pail for her.

I mean, duh. This was really dumb.

And Harry Howell, like I said, I loved him right away. A wonderful man and what a great hockey player. A Doug Barkley–type guy; had that Jean Beliveau calm and class. I thought the world of him when he was here. When he first came to our team he was already a legend and right away, first day, he put his arm around me, gave me a bit of a hug, and said, "You and I are going to get along good." And I thought, *Holy s—t, pretty nice, coming from a hotshot like that.*

Years later, when I was inducted into the Hockey Hall of Fame in 2009, Shirley and I arrived in Toronto for the ceremony. We went to check into the Hotel Toronto and who was standing at the top of the stairs as we were walking up? Harry Howell. He hugged us. His wife and Shirley had become such good friends.

So Harry Howell was the very first guy to congratulate me when I got there to be inducted. Pretty cool, huh?

Smokey McLeod was our goalie in those days. Smokey invented the hooked goalie stick. He had a club foot. But he was a great goalie. Chipper—Ron Chipperfield—was there then. George Morrison, from Toronto. Danny Lawson, good player, big hooked stick. Butch Deadmarsh. Donny Lever, I really liked Lever. But I had fun with all those guys. And, believe me, they enjoyed having fun.

BUTCH DEADMARSH
Calgary Cowboys, 1975–76, 1976–77

Bear is a great people person, was always a great supporter of the players. One thing that comes to mind is that big brawl we had in Quebec City in the playoffs when Rick Jodzio hit Marc Tardif. Tardif hit his head and was knocked out. Smokey McLeod's out there swinging his stick like a helicopter keeping people away from Rick as Curt Brackenbury and a bunch of goons are trying to get at Rick. Rick got in a lot of s—t over that but people don't realize Joe Crozier told Rick, who was a very good skater, "You're covering Tardif." Whoever's on the ice when Tardif jumps on, get off so Rick can get out there and cover him. He did come across the ice and Tardif was coming out of his own zone, a quick change, and Rick was just doing his job, gets over there, and clipped him. Tardif hit his head. Looked like he was dead. Wasn't a pretty sight. And then, as everybody knows by now, all hell broke loose.

While this all going on, the fans—just a—holes—are throwing beer over the glass and Bearcat's straddling, one foot on the bench and the other on the dasher on the boards, a stick in his hands, telling them to bugger off. Typical Bear, protecting his players. I still remember him standing there, like, "You gotta come through me!" Just defiant.

Here's another side of Bear: the one year I played on a line with Ron Chipperfield and Peter Driscoll. We had a great time. Terry Ball was one of our defencemen and he had one of the best shots of any defenceman I ever played with. Not a big guy, but he could really shoot the puck. And always four to six inches off the ice. So one day we're standing out there in the old Corral, Terry's blasting shots, and the three of us are deflecting 'em, shattering sticks. And suddenly Bearcat's screaming from the bench, "What the f—k are you guys doing?!" We'd come back to the bench for another stick after two or three shots and another broken blade. Oh, Bear went ballistic. Today that would never happen. Today, guys break 20 sticks and it doesn't matter. Here we are breaking one, two, or three, and Bear is going apeshit on us.

Another thing that sticks in my mind—he could get wound-up and a little bit nervous. One of our stupid road trips was from Calgary to Winnipeg to Cincinnati to Houston to San Diego and then to Phoenix. As I recall, the Brier was on in Calgary then, so we were gone 10 days or two weeks. So what Joe Crozier decided was to save us trooping through all these airports, he chartered a plane. Not a jet. A turbo-prop. A Fairchild, I think it was called. For maybe 35 people. So we're flying home from the game in Phoenix, end of the trip. Supposed to be three and a half, four hours to get home. We're in the air, not sure where by then, but Bearcat says, "What's that on the window?" We look, and it's oil. So he calls the flight attendant and she knows about it. We're losing oil. We had to stop three times for oil. The three-and-a-half-hour flight takes nine or 10. We get home and the sun's coming up. One of the weirdest trips I've ever been on. And Bear's freaking out. Pretty worked up. Wasn't happy at all.

So there you have three different sides to his character: Bearcat protecting his players, Bearcat giving his players s—t, and Bearcat freaking out.

Everybody remembers the crest we had on our sweaters. We'd already had some stationery made up, so one day Crozier—he had a lot on his plate at the time, of course—came up to me and said, "Geez, Bear, we need a crest. Something catchy. Something people will take a shine to. Something that's Calgary." So I told him, "Just look at the logo on our stationery and use the hat. Everything else? Gone. Only the hat."

And that's what they did. One of the best logos in the league, in my opinion.

Everyone remembers the night we had the riot in Quebec City during the 1976 playoffs. A big bench-clearing brawl. Crazy stuff. Well, Joe actually got us in that trouble by putting a boxing punching bag on the wall in our dressing room. I got the rink rats to help me do it. I knew it was gonna lead to trouble. Joe had played and coached in Quebec with the American Hockey League's Aces, so he knew all these guys working there. They're like, "What's this for?!" I told them, "Joe said we've gotta put it up."

So it gets out that we've got a punching bag in our room, a speed bag—I still have that bag; unscrewed it and brought it home with me—and the guys are training on it the day of the game! You can hear guys drumming this speed bag all over the rink.

Well, what happened later was automatic.

Rick Jodzio, a great guy, levelled Marc Tardif of the Nordiques—he was Quebec's big star—and then all hell broke loose. Legal hit by Jodzio; he ducked out from behind the defenceman and *wham*! Problem was, Tardif didn't have a helmet on in those days. Fell backward and hit his head.

So he's lying there, and, well, geez, everybody started fighting. Their players were on our bench fighting! I needed 14 stitches near my right eye after a fan kicked me in the head. I got my revenge, though. I pulled the guy's leg so his crotch came down, hard, right on the cement in the back of the players' box. So he disappeared, quick. Gone. Right in the nuts, he got it.

During this free-for-all, I looked around and Jodzio was being held by a few of their players and other guys were beating on him. So I set off to help and I saw this other fan jumping down to get a punch in on Jodzio. He was straddling our bench. Well, I just blasted him on the jaw. Down he went, then I dragged him by the scruff of the neck to the end of the bench, over to a cop, and yelled, "Get this guy outta here!"

The cop said, "I don't want him! He's all yours!" So I just left him there.

While I was doing that, that's when the guy kicked me right in the face. Oh, it was wild.

RICK JODZIO
Calgary Cowboys, 1975–77

Bear was a great trainer. Wonderful person. A solid mentor. Very experienced guy. His whole life had been spent in hockey.

At times, the coach then, Joe Crozier, could be a little on the conservative side, and Bear was a good go-between the players and the coach. You could trust him with anything. He covered everything.

You've probably heard the story of my incident with Tardif in Quebec in '76. Pretty wild night. I didn't see some of the stuff as a firsthand witness because I had my own issues at the time, but we all heard about Bear, while he was fending somebody off, grabbing Allan, who was going up into the crowd for some reason, by the seat of the pants and pulling him back onto the bench.

Management, the team, told me not to say anything. As a 21-year-old, I listened. The story was that I raced across the ice and cross-checked him to the head. It wasn't even close to that. His head was down to get the pass behind his back and I hit him with my shoulder to his chest. He fell and hit his head. Then I kinda snapped. We were right in front of the Nordiques' bench and I might've thought the Blue Wave was coming over the boards, so I jumped on him and punched him but I realized after two or three, *What the heck are you doing?*

I made amends in '07. I went to the peewee tournament in Quebec to see my son play. There was a throng of reporters there to meet our bus. For three days Tardif and I were front page. I went to his car dealership and apologized, shook his hand. I thought the whole story was overblown. I should've said my piece when it happened. I wasn't totally innocent, but it's over and done with.

Bear was very supportive through all of it. He knew that was all bulls—t. Crozier, our coach, was taunting the other team. We won the first game 3–1 in their rink, no penalties either side. So that night, Crozier's like, "What the hell are you guys doing?" So at a pregame skate, he's got me and Peter Driscoll at centre ice with boxing gloves on, along with our hockey gear. Just playing with their heads. So they come out that night running us, overreact, so when I see Tardif I think, *I'm gonna nail him*. And I over-nailed him.

My wife at the time and I spent a lot of time with Allan while we lived in Calgary. We went to the theatre with them, camped with them on the Bow River with some of the other players who hung around during the summer at the odd party or barbecue. We had a couple of decent runs in Calgary, once losing to the Winnipeg Jets in the semifinals and they ended up winning the Avco Cup. So when Bear won the Stanley Cup with the Flames I was so happy for him to have that.

Once a season, I'd go down and they'd try somebody else for a while, then I'd come back. Once, I came back to finish a road trip, a short amount of time, and I wound up as Bearcat's roommate! Back then I'd have been 21 or 22 and he would've been in his mid-forties.

He's just a solid guy. In '04, the family and I came back to visit Calgary and Banff and it was great to catch up with Allan and Bear for a coffee.

One word to describe Bearcat? The first thing that comes to mind is *resolute*. Just a strong, solid, forward-driving, consistent man.

We had a bunch of orangutans on that team, just like the first year of the Flames. A wild group. But, as I said, good guys at heart. Looking back, all my experiences to that point in my life—coming from where I had: the depression, the oil patch, the rodeo, the chuckwagons, and two little towns where people had their own ideas—really helped me in the relationship part of being a hockey trainer. I was used to all kinds of people, working with different personalities. I was lucky in that. A hotshot bronco rider is no different in their environment than a hotshot hockey player is in his.

I really enjoyed my time in the WHA. There were a lot of colourful guys playing. Honestly, I thought Crozier did well with what we had. And the city of Calgary absolutely fell in love with the team that first year. They sold standing-room season tickets. The damn rink—the Corral—was full. Then the second year, 1977, we didn't make the playoffs. Teams were coming and going in the league. And just like that, we were done. Shut the door.

That's when I jumped on a plane and went out to Vancouver, looking for a job with the Canucks. They were playing Philadelphia in a playoff series at the time and the owner there told me that when they were done their playoffs, he'd give me a call.

So I came home and WCHL owner Gerry Brisson got in touch with me and said, "Bearcat, I need a trainer." Seems he was bringing the Winnipeg Monarchs from Winnipeg into Calgary. I told him about Vancouver and he asked what they were prepared to pay me. I told him, and he said, "Oh, we can match that."

So I stayed close to home. That was the big thing for me. I didn't want to leave Okotoks, leave Calgary. No matter what. So for that to happen at the time felt like a miracle.

I had a pretty good wage, at least good enough for me. I was still in hockey. And I was home. Perfect.

Pretty much all of the guys that first year came out with the team from Winnipeg. Big Al Bellingham, who owned Mayfair Taxi in town, was my buddy and assistant bus driver. Together he went with me to Winnipeg to pick up all the crap, the equipment and such, and drive it back to Calgary.

Well, when we got to the rink, none of the guys there had been told they'd been moved! No idea. That damn Brisson never told anybody anything. Not a word.

So they're all looking at us as if we're crazy. And we said, "Well, we might be crazy but it's true. And we're loading all the stuff on the bus right now. You guys are no longer the Winnipeg Monarchs. You're now the Calgary Wranglers."

None of the players had any idea. Warren Skorodenski—Skoro—was the goalie then. An arrogant little SOB but a pretty good goalie. I remember him being p—ed off that whole first year because of the move.

You have no idea the crap that Al and I had to put up with. They got there, all the players, mumbling and grumbling—"Well, how'd you like to have that happen to you?" That kind of thing.

"Well," we told 'em, "it *did* happen. It *has* happened. So get over it."

In my three years with the Wranglers, it seemed like owners and coaches were changing every day.

Anyway, I was the guy who suggested they bring in Doug Sauter to coach. I told the owner at the time, a guy who owned a Chevy dealership up in northeast Calgary, "I know a good guy to be your coach. Doug Sauter." He was kind of an assistant coach with New Westminster at the time and came from Estevan, a good friend of Scotty's.

So I called Ernie McLean in New West and told him I had to get in touch with Sauter. He said, "Well, he's looking for a job." And I said, "Well, I'm looking for a guy."

It turned out Doug was in Calgary, and I got a call from him. He showed up in this Mustang convertible. And he had this Great Dane dog with him. He showed up at the hotel, left the convertible top down, unlocked. Brilliant. Well, someone stole his golf clubs; stole everything but the Great Dane.

Anyway, he signed that morning; became our coach.

KELLY KISIO
Calgary Wranglers, 1978–80; Calgary Flames, 1993–95

During practice with the Wranglers, instead of just watching Bearcat would also be walking the concourse on the top level of the Corral for the hour and a half, two hours we'd be on the ice. Doug Sauter used to have us on the ice forever, doing the same drill. Bearcat was—is, even now, at his age—just a man in motion. The level of energy he has is just…wrong. We should all be blessed with so much. Always going.

My back was really bugging me when I played in San Jose. So our trainer, Tom Woodcock, used to make this special liniment—he'd use horse liniment and mix it with other stuff so it was hot as hell, but a delayed hot. He'd rub this on before you went out on the ice, you'd be skating around in warm-up and all of a sudden it would hit. I mean, it worked—you'd be stiff and then the back would loosen up. But you're out there, it's running down your back and—I don't know how you'd say this—into the crack, burning like hell, and you'd be like, "Whoa!" Sure took your mind off your back, though.

So I brought this concoction with me to Calgary and told Bear, "I need this on my back." He said, "Okay."

Well, the first time Bearcat slapped it on my back before warm-up, for some reason he hadn't bothered to put on those little plastic gloves. Probably too busy doing a dozen other jobs. Anyway, I get on the ice—this is the delayed part—and I remember turning and seeing him banging his hand on the boards, hard, and yelling, "Holy crap!"

After that, he never forgot to put a plastic glove on.

CHAPTER 6

THE BIG APPLE AND COWTOWN

JOHN DAVIDSON ACTUALLY GOT ME my first NHL job. Fitting, given we'd both been part of the Centennials at the same time. Funny the way things work out.

I was still a trainer for the Calgary Wranglers at the time. Doug Sauter was coaching, and we'd just gotten beat out in the playoffs. This was spring 1980, a few months before the Flames showed up in town, and we were sitting in the dressing room in the Corral after the game, feeling sorry for ourselves and having a beer.

All of a sudden the phone rang, and Doug answered it.

"Yeah, he's here." Then he jerked his head in my direction: "Bear, you're wanted on the phone."

"By who?" I wanted to know.

And he handed me the phone and growled, "TALK!"

Well, it was J.D. calling from New York. He told me he'd heard we'd lost out, how he was sorry about that, and asked me what I'd be doing now that the Wranglers had been eliminated. I told him, "All I gotta do is take inventory, put the equipment away, and get ready for rodeo. Why? What's going on?"

Turned out, he wanted me to come to New York. Said the Rangers needed a trainer, were having a real problem with the guy they had there doing the skates. Everybody was dissatisfied with their skates.

So they wanted me to come down to do the skates and help out this trainer.

I finally said yes. Sure. Nuthin' else to do. Then he said, "That's the good news. The bad news is that your plane leaves at six in the morning." Well, this was one in the morning! But J.D. said they needed me there right away. The Rangers were getting ready for the playoffs in a week or so.

Their coach at the time was Freddie Shero. He'd won the two Stanley Cups in charge of the Philadelphia Flyers. Great guy, Freddie. Not a drop of liquor. Always coffee. We'd sit and visit. I'd tell him about rodeoing, being a jockey and all that, and he loved to hear the stories.

Thank god he was there.

Anyway, I got off the airplane in New York and there was this huge limo waiting, just for me, and the guy drove me out to Rye, where the practice rink is located. Most of the guys lived in Westchester.

For someone like me, walking into that practice rink was, well, like walking into a mansion. I mean, holy s—t, they had everything. The Rangers spent money like it was going out of style. They must've had six or seven skate sharpeners. My eyes almost popped out of my head.

One day, I see Phil Esposito walking out of the room with a dozen sticks, still wrapped in the paper. A whole damn dozen! I was used to having to account for every last stick or piece of equipment. Well, Espo saw me gawking at this and said, "Bear, this is the Rangers. You've gotta understand. We've got to spend money."

Guys had four or five pairs of skates, bags of skates, and when they'd go on a road trip, they'd take 'em all.

Anyway, that first day in New York, I walk in, cold as could be, and all these players are surprised—shocked I guess might be a better word—going, "Bear, what are you doing here?" J.D. formally introduced me and I told 'em I'd been brought in to sharpen skates.

Because the other guy was still there—and he hadn't been told I was coming—everybody was really on edge. It wasn't a comfortable situation, at least not at first.

Espo was there. J.D., of course, was too. There was Bubba Beck. That pretty boy...Ron Duguay! Don Maloney. A whole bunch of guys I already knew from juniors and the WHA. So I lucked out in that way. One of the guys I knew was Ron Greschner, the defenceman, who married supermodel Carol Alt.

A funny story about Greschner. Back when I worked for the Centennials, Greschner played for New Westminster, for Ernie "Punch" McLean. Well, Punch and I had played together in Estevan, so we knew each other well. Ernie wound up being my centreman because he wanted to win the scoring race and I could score goals.

Anyway, fast-forward to the series with Greschner, years after that. This would be, I'm guessing, in 1974. I was working with the Centennials and he was with New West, in the old Western Canada junior league. Back then, the wise guys running the show decided best-of-seven series weren't enough. No, we were going to play best-of-nine. More revenue, I guess. So, nine games, nine bench-clearing brawls. What else did they expect?

It was the same thing in the series before, against Medicine Hat. The brawls would start in that Medicine Hat series, and their guys were flipping our gloves and sticks laying on the ice up into the stands! Boy that p—ed me right off. That stuff isn't cheap. I got real tired of that.

So this started happening during the New West series too. All our crap was being flipped up and over the glass. During one brawl, in New West, I jumped out onto the ice to retrieve our stuff and put it in our bench and I started grabbing their stuff and firing it into the stands. Getting a little of our own back, right?

Next thing I knew, I look up and here came Greschner toward me. And he was mad. So was their little tough guy, Reg Duncombe. So when I saw Duncombe heading my way too, I was thinking, *Oh, s—t, this is not good.* So I jumped into our bench, grabbed three or four sticks, and started hollering, "All right, Gresch"—I knew him really well—"come on! Just try! I'm ready for you!" And I'm waving these sticks around. So Gresch grabbed Duncombe and hauled him away.

Well, that's the last time I'd seen Greschner before I got to New York. And there he was, my first day there, and I was thinking, *Uh, ohhhhhhhhh, he doesn't know I'm coming...*

But he just came over and gave me a great big hug.

There was only one guy who didn't like me, at least not at first: No. 6, defenceman Tim Bothwell. Because he was pals with the other trainer, even though this trainer was no good, as we found out. But it didn't take long and No. 6 was my friend too. It all settled down almost immediately. As I said, a lot of the players knew me already and the others realized pretty quick that I could help, because their skates were terrible.

Anders Hedberg and Ulf Nilsson both played on that team. I knew them from World Hockey when they were in Winnipeg, both great players with the Jets at the time I worked for the Calgary Cowboys. So one day Ulf, an incredible skater, came to me and said, shaking his head and muttering, "Bearcat, Bearcat...I don't need very much done on my skates but...I do not glide, I do not glide." They were grinding on the ice. So I checked the hollow and put one in that I thought would be good. I told Ulf that I had to know what he thought. He came back to me: "Better. Better."

So I kept sharpening them—a little less hollow, then a little less hollow. One day, Ulf came in and called me over, like he didn't want anyone to know. And he said, real quiet, "Bearcat, I can't hear myself skate." And I told him, "That's good." He was gliding so smooth. We both smiled. He gave me a big hug.

Boom! Then I was in good with everybody.

That was great experience for me, the time in New York, and I did a lot of work. I always seemed to be doing something at Madison Square Garden or out at the practice facility. We beat Atlanta in the first round of the playoffs that spring, then Philly took us out in the second round. During the Atlanta series we began to hear rumours that their franchise could be relocating to Calgary. We found out later that between the second and third periods of the fourth game—the night we eliminated them—Cliff Fletcher had walked into their room, really mad we were winning, and told them, "Boys, you're 20 minutes from Calgary."

Turned out, he was pretty close to right.

I've always said I went to work for the New York Rangers so we could beat Atlanta and send them to Calgary so I could get a job.

After we were done in New York, Esposito came up to me as I was getting ready to go home and told me, "Bear, when I'm general manager here—and I'm gonna be general manager here—I want you working for me." I looked at him and said, "Espo, I appreciate that. But can you see this bald-headed little potlicker from Okotoks living in New York?" He looked at me, started to laugh, and said, "Actually, no."

Then he said, "But Bear, I'm serious. Everybody here is a hockey team now. United. Together. Before, everybody was p—ing and moaning, unhappy."

And, actually, Esposito kept his word—he did call after he became general manager in New York.

But I had to tell him, "Espo, I've got the job in Calgary. This is my home. I really like it here."

He said, "I know." But he told me he'd call, and he did. Solid guy. Man of his word.

So the Rangers thing ended and I'm back home. Then comes the announcement that the Atlanta Flames are moving to Calgary. Actually, I only got the Flames job in the first place because Norm Mackie, the trainer from Atlanta when the Flames relocated, flew into town, took one look at the Corral, and said, "I'm not working here."

I'd already been turned down for the job because he was coming with the team. So I thought, *Well, that's that.*

But Norm apparently walked in the back door of the Corral, didn't even go onto the ice, stood in the hallway, and said, "This is it?! I can't work here!" then turned around and walked back out the door.

Stewie, one of the guys down at the rink, saw all this happen, watched Norm leave in a huff, and called me right away to explain what had happened.

So I was on the phone to Cliff Fletcher, the team GM, as quick as could be and told him I'd heard the trainer from Atlanta had taken one look at the Corral and left, said he couldn't work there.

Cliff didn't believe me.

I said okay, and then I told him that I was still available, still here, not going anywhere, and I'd still love to talk to him about the job if something happened.

Cliff said, pretty firmly, "He's not leaving. That can't be right. He's been with me for years."

But by god, in about two hours Cliff had called me back and said he wanted to see me. And that's how it all started.

I think Norm ended up in St. Louis. Didn't know him, not really. Big, strong guy.

A couple years later, out of the blue, I saw Cliff one day and he told me, "Your friend was just in." I had no idea who or what he was talking about. "Norm Mackie," he explained. "He's wanting his old job back. But I told him, 'No, Bear's here. And he's here to stay.'"

That first year with the Flames, boy, it was an education. Kind of like working for the Cowboys. Those WHA days were a good lead-in for me taking the Flames job.

They were all crazy. Great guys, but crazy. Willi Plett, Kenny Houston, all these huge guys, used to pick me up and throw me into the big jacuzzi. Every time I'd come up for air, to grab some breath, they'd push down on my bald head again and shove me back under the water. This went on and on. Finally they let me out. No damage done. And it wasn't anybody being mad at anybody else. Sounds awful, I know, but it was in fun—especially for them—which we did all the time. But I spent a lot my time wet, I can tell you.

I was used to the pranks, the jokes, from all the way back to when I worked as a jockey. It was a give-and-take thing.

What bothered me was the drinking. There was a lot of drinking going on. And I had to handle it. We had Al MacNeil coaching and Al was—is—a real gentleman. He treated me great. Didn't order me around, let me do my job. He treated me with respect. I had to deal with Al—"Chopper"—in order to get hired, not only Cliff. So he was an important part of the puzzle for me.

One of Al's assistants back at the start was Pierre Page. Pierre was an absolute fitness nut. I remember one time—I think it was in Colorado before they were in the NHL—we were there for an exhibition game or something. Well, the guys were out having a few beers after the game, maybe a touch after curfew, and there was Pierre, actually hiding behind one of those potted palm trees in the lobby of the hotel, peeking to see who was coming in late. I mean, crazy.

I don't know whose idea that was—his or Chopper's—and never did find out, but it wasn't a good one. The guys had a lot of fun with that.

PAUL REINHART
Calgary Flames, 1980–88

When I think of Bearcat I think back to the beginnings of the NHL in the west, the innocence and naiveté. We forget when we look at the game today and how sophisticated it is at all levels that it was brand-new to Western Canada in the early '80s. Certainly to the prairies. Back then, it was still incredibly important to have local connections in the organization that linked it to the community. That revolved around players and other personnel in the summertime staying in the cities and helping market the team. A lot of us didn't just come to Calgary to play, we moved in and made our lives there. Adding to the ties was our strong local ownership and our connection to Hockey Canada.

Bearcat, being so well-known in the community and around the province, exemplified what I'm talking about. Add the type of person he was, so outgoing, so ready to volunteer…to me just demonstrated how important that connection really was. Bearcat was Calgary through and through. You thought of Calgary, you thought of Bearcat. Automatically.

During the years I was there, and particularly the early ones, Bearcat was as much a part of growing that organization in many respects as any of the players. That should never be underestimated.

I think I enjoyed good relationships with just about everybody down through the years, including the assistant coaches. Guy Charron was a real good guy. Guy Lapointe, a helluva defenceman in Montreal, was so funny. Such a joker, playing pranks. We had more fun than I can tell you. We'd be on the bench during warm-up, and Guy would nudge me and kind of nod up into the crowd. "Hey, Bear, third row, white sweater, 45 degrees over. Check her out." And then he'd say something in French, *sacre bleu!* or something like that, and we'd laugh and laugh. We'd be doing that the whole warm-up.

And the media guys, we always had such a good time together. Doug Barkley and Peter Maher, of course. They would always invite Bobby Stewart and me out to eat so we were never alone, and in our job it could get kind of lonely.

DOUG BARKLEY
Calgary Flames radio colour commentator, 1980–2002

On the road, Bearcat was a shopaholic, always on the lookout for bargains. In Boston, he'd go to Filene's Basement for the deals. They'd put all the stuff you'd buy in brown paper bags. Being a small guy, Bear's size was easy to get. One time he bought two suits, supposed to be Italian suits, at Filene's, and we're walking back to the hotel when this gentleman crosses the streets carrying this lovely big garment bag. We kind of fall into step with this guy and I say to him, "Geez, I see you bought a couple suits. Like my friend here." He looks at Bear, with this folded-up paper bag rolled up under his arm, and says, "I don't think so."

Another time we're in L.A. Bear runs into me and says, "Geez, Bark, you should go over. I found a place where there's a great deal on vodka—like $3.95 a bottle."

"Holy cow, that's great, Bear." But, really, $3.95 a bottle....

Well, to get what he'd bought back into the country, he has Pete, Bobby, me, and some others to help declare it. So he gets back and puts the vodka in the freezer to keep it cold. Well, the vodka froze. Solid. Hardly any alcohol in it. All water.

So many people around the city came to him for treatments. He'd do anything for anybody. That's why he's so well-known. Another thing about him, he'd play in 60 to 70 golf tournaments a summer for the Flames, as the auctioneer, then on a hole he'd hit shots and everyone would hit from that spot. We travelled a lot together, driving to charity golf tournaments over the years.

While he was alive, Bear's dad would drive in from Okotoks for the games. He had Bear's seats and he wouldn't leave the rink until Pete and I waved to him from the press box. Sometimes we'd get busy and forget. So we'd be getting ready to leave, half hour or so after the game sometimes, look down, and his dad would still be sitting there, waiting for us to wave.

And such a great family man. When Bearcat retired, the Flames players got together and gave him and his wife two weeks in Hawaii. At the time, he and Shirley were looking after Danny's kids. So they turned the trip down. They didn't want anyone else looking after the kids.

PETER MAHER
Calgary Flames play-by-play broadcaster, 1981–2014

Bearcat and I were inducted into the Alberta Sports Hall of Fame the same night in May 2015, in Red Deer. It's believed he set a record for longest acceptance speech. And it actually brought about a change in procedure! On a night with a dozen other inductees, he spoke for 27 minutes and would've continued on (and on) if MC Grant Pollock hadn't interceded.

As always, Bearcat regaled us with some great stories, but time was a factor on a busy night, what with the other 11 people being enshrined plus a couple of live auction segments with a number of great fundraising items. I had to speak soon after he did. Try following that.

The original plan was for Grant and me to do a Q&A. When it came time, Grant whispered to me, "Uh, we have to keep this short. Very short…"

From that night on, inductees were told the acceptance speeches could be no more than three minutes long and organizers wanted a copy of the speeches a couple of days in advance. Later, I noted, "Bearcat was told to speak for three minutes, but he thought he'd heard 30 minutes. So he actually had three minutes to spare."

Not only did Bearcat get players with injuries and illness ready for games but he also provided a great assist in helping me have a career where I never missed a game. If on the day of a game I had the flu, a cold, or a hangover, I'd go see Bearcat. He always had a remedy for me that helped me get through the night.

He'd spice up our broadcasts, too. Can't count how many times I'd be interviewing a player in the dressing room and he'd happen to pass by after a team victory and start yodelling in the background. Even when he was retired he'd come by our broadcast booth during a game and give us a little yodel.

Besides the guys who travelled with us regularly, we had a great group of media in Calgary. Ken Newans. Jim Hughes. Billy Powers. Real personalities. All such wonderful people. I go all the way back to Henry Viney, for cripes' sake!

And during the Centennials days, we had Dick Chubey writing for *The Albertan*. Now there was a character. Dick would saunter into Scotty's office after games, plop into Scotty's chair, and he'd just down the booze. The last guy to leave, Chubes. Just a son-of-a-gun.

One player who I loved like a brother almost right away the first year of the Flames was our big defenceman, Phil Russell, who'd played against us in juniors when he was with the Edmonton Oil Kings. I hung out with him. He really protected me.

That first year, Kent Nilsson had an amazing season: 131 points, which remains a franchise record. The Magic Man, everybody called him, and it was true. He was just a treat to watch. Even in practice you couldn't take your eyes off him. And a nice, relaxed guy. What a talent!

People always talk about hockey then versus hockey now. Well, I think Kent could've played in any era. Remember, when we had him the game was damn tough. Hard. Mean. Pretty much anything goes. Yet he still excelled.

I really used to get ticked off when people would call him soft, a floater, hiding in the corners. I thought he was awesome. He could do anything with the puck. Some of the tricks…you'd sit back and shake your head, just amazed.

People ask me a lot about the Corral, what it was like. Well, I'd had a lot of experience in there by the time the Flames came to town—I actually played in the first game ever in the building, in 1950 with the Okotoks Oilers. I was still a snot-nosed kid going to school. I know because I had had a bit of an argument with the guy from Molsons, Stu Hendry, who was the goalie for the Stampeders in those days, about who was the first team to play. He claimed they were the first ones, but the Oilers—we weren't in the Big Six at the time—played an exhibition, the first game of a doubleheader in there on the Sunday. The Stampeders played on the Monday. Stu checked it out and told me, "You little SOB, you were right!"

The big arena before the Corral was built was the old Victoria Arena, where the Saddledome sits now.

In 1950 it was state-of-the-art, but by time the Flames arrived it was a barn. It was always jammed, though, standing-room season tickets like we used to have with the Cowboys. And the boards were so damned high. That's something everybody remembers.

That first year of the Flames we had a really good run in the playoffs, beat Chicago and then Philly. That Philly series was quite the upset. We had an experienced group, but the guys hadn't had a lot of success as a team before in Atlanta. It was kind of a fly-by-night thing in Atlanta. The Flyers couldn't push us around—we had a big, tough team—and we wound up winning Game 7 right in the Spectrum. They got a little crazy and we scored a few power-play goals, as I remember.

That Skalbania, boy, he pulled a fast one in buying the team in the first place. The Calgary guys—Harley Hotchkiss, Doc, and B.J. Seaman, along with Normie Kwong—were originally making the deal with Atlanta owner Tom Cousins, and somehow Skalbania got in there and bought the team out from underneath them. Stole it. Very upsetting to everybody.

Right away, first thing Skalbania did, as I remember, was make a deal with CBC Television and sold them all the rights to the games. So he made a s—tload of money right there, probably more than he paid for the team. And, of course, he ended up selling his stake to our gang and made a whole bunch of money there. So he cleaned up twice!

Quite a skullduggery deal that he pulled on them, in my opinion.

Skalbania didn't know a thing about hockey. He was strictly a businessman.

Our group, the Calgary gang...well, you couldn't find nicer, more down-to-earth people. Before I got into the training business, I worked in the oil patch and did a lot of work with the Seaman brothers' oil company, in the drilling rigs. They were in Saskatchewan. When Shirley and I got married and were living in Estevan, we rented a home there. The superintendent of the drilling company moved in upstairs. His name was Doug Gamble. He and his wife, Opal, became very, very good friends of ours. Then we moved to Estevan, and Doug took over Doc Seaman's ranch in Millarville. We'd go out and visit and I'd do a lot of deer hunting and elk hunting on their land.

So when they all came together and wound up owning the hockey team, everybody was happier'n hell.

Harley and Becky Hotchkiss, all of them, were absolutely great to us. When they'd be on the road with the team, Harley and Becky would take the whole damn bunch of us out for dinner, in old-town Quebec City and places like that. Wonderful times. But that's the kind of people they were. They cared about you.

They'd have parties at their house for everyone. They befriended the country singer from Longview, Ian Tyson. So he'd be there many, many times when they'd invite the whole team out to their big house in Southwest Calgary. Big swimming pool, the whole thing.

The way those owners treated us was incredible. They loved all of us and we loved them. What an organization at that time! Then, having Cliff Fletcher as GM, running the show, well, you couldn't ask for more support. Everything was first-class. Whatever you needed to help make the team better or someone feel more comfortable, you got.

CLIFF FLETCHER
Calgary Flames general manager, 1980–90

When I arrived in Calgary in 1980 it was the Monday of Victoria Day Weekend. I had to rush up there because Nelson Skalbania had an off-the-cuff press conference saying we were going to announce not only the team but if that anybody wanted to bring their money down the Corral, we'd be happy to take it.

So I get there, check into the hotel and who's the first person sitting in the lobby, waiting to meet me, wanting to talk to me?

Bearcat.

This was my first trip to Calgary in years, and I had no idea who Bearcat was. I said to him, "Oh, and what do you do?" He said, "I'm going to be your athletic trainer." And I kinda looked at him. "Oh, you are, are you? And what might your name be?"

We talked. To say the least, Bear was a real extrovert. Only after asking a few questions around the city did I begin to understand what a personality he was and how well-respected. An amazing guy. He operated in a different era, remember. The sophistication that goes into being an athletic therapist or a trainer these days is worlds different than the days when Bearcat was in charge. But to me you only judge by the bottom line. And the bottom line with Bearcat was: boy, did players recover from injuries quickly. He was way ahead of his time as far as treating players went.

I'll never, ever forget that night he ran out onto the ice against L.A. in the playoffs and we scored that goal! I laugh like hell about it now but at the time, if they hadn't counted that goal, I would've killed him.

Now when I'm asked about it, I just tell people, "Well, Bearcat's the only trainer in NHL history who's plus-1!"

One of the great things about that first year of the Flames for me was teaming up with Bobby Stewart, our equipment manager. He came with the team from Atlanta, with Cliff. We couldn't have been more different as people but we just hit it off. Can't tell you why, exactly. Probably because he was just a wonderful guy, Bobby. You don't meet many like him, anywhere.

There were some hair-raising nights getting equipment to the next town, I'll tell you. One time we were getting on the airplane, somewhere in the Southern U.S.—we were flying commercial back then, remember, and I always used to position myself on the right-hand side of the plane so I could watch them loading the equipment. Well, it's going on, like usual. I turned away for a second, turned back, and the next thing I know it was coming off. Being unloaded!

Well, we had a game in another city the next day. So I found assistant coach Pierre Page on the plane and told him, "We've got a problem. A big problem." Can you imagine the fine if we'd shown up for a game with no equipment?

So Pierre hightailed it up to talk to the pilot, and he explained to Pierre that they had to take our equipment off because there would be no room underneath for the mail. So Pierre told the pilot, "If that's the case, there's no room for us, either. We're outta here." Then he went back into the cabin and told the guys, "Okay, everybody up! We're off the plane." Well, boom, the s—t hit the fan, guys started getting up to leave, and pretty soon the equipment was being loaded back on.

But that's the kind of crazy stuff Bobby and I had to deal with.

I don't think in all the years we worked together that we ever had an argument, which, considering how much work we had to do and how much time we spent together late nights and early mornings at all those arenas, is pretty amazing.

I do remember I was always after him to stop drinking all that Coca-Cola. Then, later, he got diabetes and it wound up killing him. So sad.

Like I said, Bobby and I got along great. We were a team. I just loved the guy.

The second season, Badger Bob arrived as coach. College guy, college ways. Looking back, I don't think there was any actual problem between him and me. Mainly because I was smart enough to behave myself. But for me personally, he was the toughest coach I ever worked for.

I thought he was an excellent, excellent practice coach—he absolutely *loved* practice—but on the bench during games…it could get wild. Poor old Mud, Bob Murdoch, got all the s—t. We'd have a goal scored on us and Badger would yell, "What happened, Mud?"

71

Because he loved practice so much, we—Bobby and I—never got a day off. Maybe three guys would go out on the ice, but someone always had to, and we'd have to be there for them. He'd tell us, "You guys are getting paid to be here, so be here."

He was always bringing guys in to do different exercises and stuff, but in doing that players were getting injured, pulling different muscles and things like that. He was always saying. "Tape an aspirin on it and get your a— out there!" These guys were fighting for their hockey lives, right? So they weren't going to say no.

TIM HUNTER
Calgary Flames, 1982–92

I had a serious problem one time. The bursa sac on my elbow was inflamed. Our doctor at the time, Pete McMurtry, said it doesn't seem to be much. So we practiced, I went home to get my stuff—we were flying somewhere at five or six o'clock, commercial flights in those days. Go home, get your gear, get to the airport to Vancouver or wherever.

By the time I got home, I've got this red line down my forearm. Weird. My wife took a look and said, "That is not good." So I called Bearcat and he told me to get to the Holy Cross and Terry Groves would meet me there. Turned out I had blood poisoning. As soon as I mentioned that line on my arm Bear was like, immediately, "Get your a— to the hospital." He knew. He was ready. If I got on that flight thinking it was something else, I would've died. But Bear was on top of it and obviously Terry Groves was, too.

We saw him as this father figure who had our best interests at heart; more than a trainer to us.

He'd hold a Hot Stove Lounge in his office at the rink. We never had beer in the dressing room in Calgary, but Bear had a few in a little fridge there. "C'mon in and have a little nick-nick," he'd say. So you'd be sitting

72

around with Bear and Pep or Lanny or Brad McCrimmon, whoever was around, having a sip and chewing the fat before you went home.

Bearcat was that old-school guy from a different era. Things were starting to change with the new fitness and everything. He was one of those come-to-training-camp-to-get-in-shape guys. But he was always in shape, doing something like bringing the bike over to the glass and riding when we were on the ice.

Bear was seeing a lot of changes in the game at the time. Some of it he turned his nose up at, but he was progressive, as well.

I knew Badger wasn't all that happy with me because I wasn't a college graduate. That was a big deal to him. I guess we were from two different worlds. But I know B.J. Seaman and Harley Hotchkiss and the owners stuck up for me and we got through it. I think Badger regretted having me around, but he couldn't do anything about it.

As I said, he was really partial to college guys. If you weren't a college guy, he seemed to ignore you. Which is why we couldn't figure why he treated one of our hardest-working players, Colin Patterson, the way he did for a while.

Well, Colin had gone to Clarkson College, but for a time there Badger absolutely ignored him in the room, on the bench. He'd walk down the line in the dressing room going, "You're playing. You're playing. You're playing," then come to Colin and walk right past him without a word! Just like that.

Patter, a real easygoing guy, would just shrug his shoulders. So I told Colin one time, "I've just nicknamed you The Ghost." And he said, "What the hell is that all about?" So I told him, "Well, that's what you are. Badger doesn't see you. You're invisible!" Well, he looked at me and started to laugh. I told him, "Keep your head up. One of these days he's going to need you because you're a helluva hockey player and he's finally going to see you, like some great big saviour coming over a hill on a big horse."

And that's exactly what happened. Somebody got hurt before a game and I came into the room after warm-up, saw Colin, and winked at him. Then Badger came in and I told him this other guy—can't remember who it was—couldn't play. No way.

So Badger walked down the line as usual, strolled by Patter before he stopped dead in his tracks, gradually turned around, then pointed at Colin. "Patterson! Patterson! Patterson! *There you are! You're playing tonight!*"

Well, Patter just winked at me and I had to get the hell out of there because I was going to fold up on the floor.

Badger was gone by 1989 when we won, of course, but I've watched our Game 6 in Montreal a few times over the years and I can't believe how outstanding a game Patterson played that night. I mean, he was *awesome*. Every time I watch that game he gets better.

By then, of course, everybody could see The Ghost and what a fine player he was.

I always tried to stay in as good a physical condition as possible. That'd been the way I was brought up and if I was asking these players to be fit, how could I not show a good example? That's why I always exercised and rollerbladed around the Saddledome and in whatever rink we'd be at on the road.

JAMIE MACOUN
Calgary Flames, 1983–92

When I got to Calgary, I was 21 and Bearcat was 45, if he was a day. But he always tried to stay in shape. I remember walking into the medical/training room and he's standing there, no shirt on, wearing these tiny—and I mean tiny—little red shorts. Man...that was definitely something you didn't need to see early in the morning.

One time I'd hurt my elbow in the previous game and I said to him, "Hey, Bear, get dressed and take a look at this, will ya?" And he looked at me funny and hollered, "I am dressed!"

He used to rollerblade around the concourses of all the rinks where were playing and he'd wear this Walkman headset, listening to music. We were at the old Checkerdome in St. Louis one time, and in those days only equipment manager Bobby Stewart and Bear made the trips. Of course, somebody gets hurt—can't remember who it was—and we're all yelling for Bear. *Where's Bear?! Where's Bear?!* But he's got his headset on, and those little red shorts, and he's skating around the concourse.

Not an emergency, luckily. But it must've taken us five minutes to flag him down.

In those days, everybody had just gone nuts about fitness. And in a lot of instances with the players, they wound up going overboard. There is a balance between enough and too much. They had a thing called 3D, found it in a book somewhere—say you're doing sit-ups, then you'd have another player planted *on top of you,* and then the poor guy doing the sit up would have to complete it. Again and again and again. I'd say, "Whoa! Whoa! Whoa!" They were actually injuring players trying to maximize their fitness. And those players wound up missing games and then would be complaining to me.

That was really upsetting. The intention was right but...too much. And I'm just the trainer. I mean, lay down on your stomach to do your back lifts and somebody's sitting on you with their big, fat a—s on your shoulders and you've got to lift them up?

That was really tough to watch, but I had to deal with it.

So, unfortunately, did the guys who matter most—the players.

CHAPTER 7

MOVE TO THE DOME

IN 1983 WE MOVED ACROSS THE STREET and into the Saddledome. After the years at the Corral, the place seemed like a palace.

While they were working on getting it finished, though, Bobby and I would have to visit the office of the builder and go over certain things, inspect what was going to be our dressing room. When we'd find things wrong, we were asked to report the problems. Many things they just tore out and redid. Other things they added to the blueprints on our recommendation.

But if you go in there now and get a chance to look under the roof, it's just amazing the place stood up. I remember, as an example, our dressing room. My trainer's room was right next to the coaches' office. The coaches had a real nice shower and bathroom right there, in their office. They were happier'n hell. Right beside it, I had these little cement pits made that would hold water, maybe six inches high, and I had my whirlpools inside that kind of a tub. Well, there were supposed to be fault-breakers inside the wall for the electricity and stuff, because of all the water around. They had wires coming out of the wall! Regular plugs like you and I would have in our house! Very dangerous.

So I had to go back and explain what we needed. I mean, I told 'em, "I've got these tubs in there full of water, and I've got to drain 'em every day. Show me where the drain is?"

No drains! In the whole dressing room.

They had clean-outs, as they called them, but you couldn't be putting fluids down there because they'd go right through there and out into the Elbow River.

I had to make 'em tear the thing out and do a rebuild. So they punched a hole through the wall into the coaches' shower and we drained the whirlpool through the coaches' shower all the time we were there, if you can believe it. The coaches were p—ed off, because they'd be in there and I'd be draining ice-cold water. Just asinine, the way it was done.

I know Gary Taylor had a lot of challenges electrically because he was in charge of the video when we got in there. The wiring…there were so many wires in the ceiling they didn't know which one was going where, so whenever they fixed anything they'd just put in a new wire. So anytime you'd have to look up there, it was like staring at a bird's nest.

But it was new, all the whistles and bells, and had lots of room. A big, big upgrade from the Corral, obviously.

Still, I honestly don't know how they ever got that thing up. Amazing.

JOEL OTTO
Calgary Flames, 1985–96

Just a man-of-all-trades, Bearcat. He was somebody you could talk to, who could calm you down, who could pump you up, who took care of you. You believed in what he was doing.

I remember the first time I was going into Minnesota, back home, to play against the North Stars at the Met Centre. All pumped up. Back in the day, Sudafed was just becoming popular. I'd heard that they might help you play better and I wanted to be at my best in Minnesota. So I went and asked Bear for Sudafed.

He asked me, "Are you sick?" I told him, "No, we're going into Minnesota. My home state. I want to play well." And so on. And he wouldn't let me take them.

We all had that trusted-family-doctor type relationship with him. He was—and this is actually way more important than it sounds—a comfort.

Chapter 8

The Rise:
Battle Lines Drawn,
March to the Finals

THE BATTLE OF ALBERTA was at its height then, in the '80s.

The Edmonton Oilers were the kings—had so many great, great players, so it felt like we were always trying, and failing, to catch up.

Seemed like every time we played against Edmonton, I'd be stitching up two, three, four guys. The doctor they had up there was a great guy. Good thing, too. Because a lot of players needed attention during those games. Boy, I must've used hundreds and hundreds of stitches in games against the Oilers.

There were so many fights, it was quite honestly hard to keep track. One that comes to mind, later on, is the one between Stu Grimson and Dave Brown. Stu had done a great job in a fight between the two of them up at Edmonton a couple nights earlier. He'd embarrassed Brown. So you knew, I mean you *knew*, Brown would be coming right after him, looking for revenge. In the days leading up to the next game, I kept reminding him, "Stewie, this guy's madder'n hell. Don't let your guard down, even in warm-up!"

And Stewie just kept saying, "Yeah, okay Bear, you're right."

And then what happened? Brown lined up beside Stewie, he dropped his gloves before the puck hit the ice, and *pow!* A really one-sided fight. And I was so p—ed off! 'Cause it wasn't as if Stewie hadn't been warned. And not just by me.

People always ask me to pick one highlight from all my years as a trainer in the NHL, and everyone expects me to say the night we won the Stanley Cup in Montreal. That's the obvious one, of course. And it was totally amazing, don't get me wrong.

But beating the Oilers in the playoffs in '86 has just got to be at the very top of my list. My greatest thrill in hockey. I have pictures of me jumping in the air at the end of Game 7 in Edmonton. Not because I hated the Oilers, the way you were supposed to. But because they were so good; because beating them was such a great achievement. They were the best and we'd just beaten the best.

I mean, I went nuts.

The goal that won it for us everybody remembers, the one where Oilers defenceman Steve Smith's pass went in off Grant Fuhr's left leg. It took most everybody by surprise. I mean, Perry Berezan, who got credit for the goal, didn't even see it because he'd already come back to the bench, wasn't even on the ice!

But I had a real good view.

Fuhr was way out in front of the net instead of being on the post, where he should've been. When the pass deflected in off him, nobody could quite believe what had just happened. The rink went absolutely silent.

Smitty took a lot of heat for that afterward, really got roasted in the newspapers, but I told him one time, while he was still with the Oilers, "You didn't score that goal! I'm the opposition, remember, and I'm here to tell you—that wasn't your fault."

He and I became very good friends after that. By the time he came to play for us—and who at that time—'86—would've ever thought an Oiler would ever be wearing a Flames jersey!—I was in my ambassador job, and one day we got to talking. He remembered my saying what I had, defending him, and he told me, "Bear, you have no idea how good you made me feel when you came and told me that." Which made me feel pretty darn good because he's a heckvua guy.

So, tough on Smitty, for sure, but like I said, winning that series tops my list.

Other memories involving the Oilers aren't so sweet. I remember losing that playoff series to them in '88—we were swept in four straight after winning the President's Trophy for the first time—and flying back on the plane, crying like a baby, tears just streaming down my cheeks. I was sitting beside Cliff at the time and he must've thought I was absolutely crazy. But it was just a release of emotion. Playing against Edmonton, the highs seemed higher and the lows lower than at any other time.

There were two or three of their guys, maybe, who always p—ed me off. The little guy who was such a SOB with his stick, Ken Linseman, for one. The Rat. Hated him. Glenn Anderson, too.

But the tough guys, no. Guys like Marty McSorley, Dave Semenko. They were just doing their job. And the rest of them were good with me. I was amazed, given how tough the games ended up being, but we got along quite well, me and the Oilers. Their players, Glen Sather, all of 'em, treated me like a king. I'd go in their dressing room for stuff. Not like I was spying or anything. I knew them all.

People just couldn't believe that back then. Still can't. To this day, I'll go golfing with a guy in the summer, for instance, at some charity event, and he'll say, trying to provoke me, "Well, I'm an Oilers fan." And my automatic reply was, still is, "So am I!" And then I'll tell him stories about their players, those days, and those guys would just stand there on the tee or in the fairway with their mouths open.

They thought they'd get me going, that I was going to react, get mad. But I told them the way it was.

* * *

Some crazy stuff happened in games against the Oilers. And not all of it on the ice.

One guy made all our crests—he was really good at it—but he screwed up this one time. Brand-new set of jerseys and we head up to

Edmonton. I left the jerseys there at the rink to wash, first time to be worn, that night.

And they all turned pink. Yes, pink.

The backing on the crest was the wrong material. He didn't know it. We go to start the game and they're pink. It's in the papers and everything—pink jerseys. Imagine. Now, of course, teams wear pink jerseys to show support for initiatives. But back then...*pink* jerseys?! In Edmonton, of all places?!

Well.

Bobby just peed his pants.

Usually the crest guy did a really good job for us. After we got involved with him, everybody else started taking their stuff to him. But I'll never forget the pink jerseys. Still have a couple, in my basement somewhere.

Gretzky? Good guy. If I needed something, he'd invite me into their room before a game, while they were getting dressed. "C'mon in Bear, no problem."

But, looking back, every team was like that with us trainers. We were treated like family. Just awesome. I suppose it was the nature of the job.

That year, '86, Cliff made some tremendous additions to the team. Joey Mullen. Nick Fotiu. Not only were these guys great players—Mullen scored so many big goals for us I wouldn't know where to start—but they fit in so well too. Which means so much to a team.

How Cliff got Mullen in the first place, I'll never know. Sure glad he did, though. But that was Cliff. He made trades that made a big difference.

Quiet guy, Joey, but an amazing talent. And a tough little SOB, in his way. Didn't matter how many times you'd knock him down, he just kept getting up. And then he'd score the big goal. He'd always get the last laugh.

Nick was a great practical joker. Big guy, super tough, from New York. I'd put out this little dish with melted wax and oil, and the guys would soak their hands in it for injuries and things. Well, that got Nick to thinking. He started coming to practice with a bunch of doughnuts. He'd dip them in the wax and then set them out. Of course, the guys would come in, licking their lips, and say, "Yeah! Doughnuts!" and start chomping away on the wax.

Nicky also came in one day with me, early, and grabbed all the towels. He had a spray-can of whipped cream with him. So he ordered me, "Bearcat, don't say a damned thing!" Okay. My lips are sealed. He then took the towels and sprayed whipped cream between every one of them and put 'em on the rack. Well, the guys hopped out of the shower later, not paying any attention, and started to dry themselves off. Whipped cream all over 'em!

Some of the guys were ticked off, some were laughing like hell, but it worked like a darn. And Nick was so nonchalant about the whole thing, played the part so well—he didn't do this, how dare anyone accuse him, etc., etc. Completely deadpan.

That's the kind of guys they were. We had fun every single day.

JAMIE HISLOP
Calgary Flames, 1980–83; assistant coach, scout

When the Olympics were in Calgary in 1988, Katarina Witt was the gold medalist in women's figure skating. And a stunning-looking woman, as everyone knows.

Well, a couple of years later, she came into town to film this big Coke commercial at the 'Dome. So they had the ice put back in the Saddledome. I was working down there in development with the Flames at the time. Bearcat always seemed to be down there, paddling around.

Anyway, Katarina Witt is there doing this one jump for the commercial, trying to land it, trying to land it. And she keeps falling. Now she injures herself and she needs some help. She's hurt a hip. Someone tells her the Flames trainer is in the dressing room and asks, could he help? She says sure.

Well, the ol' Potlicker, he's rubbing his hands together. So she comes in, they get the introductions over with, and Katarina Witt tells him, "I've hurt my hip. Is there anything you can do?" And he says, "Well, I can give you a little massage, a rubdown." She says okay, and I guess she just pulled down her leotard and hopped right up on the training table. Well, Bearcat was just a-grinnin'. And he gave Katarina Witt a massage. In his glory. True story.

He was really old-school. He'd try and rub out a charley horse or whatever using a quarter. The modern guys just put the gel on and use ultrasound. And here's Bearcat's rubbing it out with a quarter or a silver dollar. But, let me tell you, it worked.

He was pretty innovative, too, though. As an example, he was the one who first invented those little track cleats—put them on the bottom of his shoes so he wouldn't be slipping and sliding if he had to rush out on the ice to help somebody.

That was Bearcat. Always thinking. And just such a good guy. He put a bulletin board up behind his desk. Different guys were married and starting families, first child a lot of times, and they'd bring the kids into the dressing room. Bear would always take pictures, using one of those old instant cameras where the photo developed in front of our eyes, and he'd put the picture of you and your baby up on the bulletin board. Stuff like that. Just a really neat guy.

As I said, we were lucky enough to have a lot of jokers around in those early years of the Flames. So the rest of the guys would play up to the antics. Our goalie, Reggie Lemelin, was a genuinely funny, free-spirited guy. He used to get dressed up in a Santa Claus suit, sit on the table in the middle of the room, and act as the judge in a kangaroo court.

And he'd make guys do all kinds of stuff. I still have videos of those. They were hilarious.

When I worked for Oil Well in Calgary years before, we had a lady who would make sure that everyone received a card on their birthday. Without fail. So when I began training, I kept up the tradition.

With the Flames we had this big whirlpool, so I'd take a bunch of foam, thick, and shape it into a boat with three or four levels and then on top I'd stick a tongue depressor as a mast, then overtop of that I'd put the guy's number, like a candle on a cake. And every morning somebody would be celebrating a birthday, he'd walk in with one of these in the whirlpool, floating around. Then I'd put HAPPY BIRTHDAY on the bulletin board, in English for the English-speaking guys and French for the French-speaking guys.

Another one of those big moves that year was the trade for John Tonelli from the Islanders. We gave up a couple of great people, Steve Konroyd and Richie Kromm, in that deal. But Tonelli had been on those four-in-a-row Islanders Stanley Cup teams and he had experience beating the Oilers.

Bobby called it the Shopping Cart Trade. They came to tell us in the morning that the trade had been made. We happened to be on Long Island for a game that night and we used a shopping cart to take all the equipment from the two guys we gave up down the hall to the Islanders' room and bring Tonelli's equipment back to our room. I'd never seen that before.

After we beat the Oilers that year we got all the way to the final. It was tough to lose to the Canadiens. You get that close and can't finish the deal, it hurt. Hurt like hell.

A lot of people also remember that Oilers series because that's the time I went into the stands after my son and assistant trainer, Allan—Game 1, in Edmonton—and hurt my ankle.

What happened was this: Gary Suter got hit out in front of our bench and his stick went flying over the glass, into the crowd. There were two

91

young guys, fans, who grabbed the stick and put it down by their feet, under the seat. First thing I know, Allan's gone over the glass to retrieve the stick and he's started to wrestle with these guys.

So I hightailed it out of the players' box, underneath the stairs. Well, the stairs were covered, so I came running back on the bench and by now it looked to me like Allan was in big trouble. I jumped up and over the glass and came down on the stairway and one foot landed on the step. The other one missed and down I went. Meantime, Allan had retrieved the stick and he was back on the bench. I'm lying there thinking my leg's broke. So I climbed over the glass and dropped down on the bench, on my hands and knees, crawling along, trying to get off. Well, Crispie comes along and he started kicking me. "Get out of the way! Get out of the way! You're in my way!" Well, I kept on crawling and finally everybody realized I was in trouble.

A couple of people—can't remember who—grabbed me and took me out down the tunnel and there was a paramedic there. He fired me onto a wheeled stretcher. Well, I wound up in the dressing room and the doctors were looking me over. All this time, the doggone TV camera had been following me and the red light was on, meaning I knew I was on TV. Live. So I started blowing kisses at the camera.

The ambulance was parked at the back of the arena, in the open space by the loading dock. They wheeled me down there and the camera guy was walking right beside me with the camera up on his shoulder. I looked out onto the ice through the Zamboni entrance and the game was still going on. But they were still filming me! So I threw more kisses.

Well, away we went to the hospital. I can remember being wheeled by all these people on beds in the hallway there. I was thinking, "Oh, boy, now I'm causing a lot of trouble…" The doctors took X-rays and there turned out to be no break, just torn ligaments in the ankle. So they threw a cast on it and said, "Get him out of here!" So we went back to the rink, game's still on, I had the cast and crutches and I hobbled out to the players' box and back to the bench and we finish up the game.

THE RISE: BATTLE LINES DRAWN

And that was how the Bearcat Murray Fan Club in Boston was born. These fans were watching the game on ESPN down there, had seen me go into the crowd after Allan—I'm pretty sure they'd had a few pops—and decided, *That's our guy! He's our hero!*

I found out about it pretty quick and talked to a few of them on the phone. Then I kind of forgot about them. Well, the first time we went to play in Boston the next season, they were in the bar—The Penalty Box Lounge—before the game, across the street from the old Garden. That was their hangout. So I knew they were going to be there and I told Grant Pollock, the host of the local TV broadcasts, about these guys. I said, "They're are all going to be in the bar and they'd love to see you." So Grant went over there with his camera guy. And they televised it back home, talking to these guys, the story about how and why the fan club had been started. The whole thing. Grant did a great job.

GRANT POLLOCK
Calgary 7 Flames TV host, 1986–2000

Bearcat was always helpful to the traveling Calgary media whenever we needed a hand. I know play-by-play man Ed Whalen needed him on many occasions when Ed fell ill. Bearcat would always come up with a magic potion to fix him up, especially on game day. The exchange usually played out like a drug deal in a back alley, taking place early in the morning inside the cramped visitors' dressing room.

One time I remember needing help in Chicago during the '96 playoffs. I came down with the flu and on the day between games I couldn't get out of bed I was so sick.

So I stayed in my room at the Drake Hotel for 24 hours, passing interviews (disastrously, as it turned out) off on a small, cranky newspaper writer. The next day, game day, I literally had no voice—far less than ideal for someone who makes his living talking.

However, I did manage to drag my sorry a— to the rink in order to do a pregame hit live on TV. I stopped by the dressing room on the way and knowing my condition, Bearcat gave me a huge mug of the secret potion he'd always whip up for Ed to fix laryngitis.

It tasted terrible. I think it was mostly hot steamy vinegar and tea and something else. Anyway, it made me heat up and I was sweating, which also isn't a good thing for anyone going on air. Still, I have to admit the magic elixir helped in the short term; my voice was good enough to make it through the live hit from the United Center and I managed to get through the rest of the night in half-decent shape.

Without Bearcat's concern and taking time to help me out, I might not have been able to go on the air that evening. He literally gave me my voice back.

That whole night, when the fan club showed up, was kind of surreal. During warm-up, at that old rink there was so little room we had to stand in Boston's players' box to watch our guys to our left down at the other end of the rink.

Warm-up's going on, then Charlie Simmer, playing for Boston at the time, came sliding along with his elbow on the boards, gave me a nudge, and said, "I didn't know you had relatives down here, Bear."

Huh?

I said, "I don't."

I'd been watching our guys during the warm-up, not paying attention to anyone else. With the game coming up, I'd forgotten all about the fan club.

So Charlie went off, took a shot on goal, skated back, and told me, "Well, there's a whole bunch of them here. Your relatives."

I was like, "What do you mean?"

Then he jerked his head up toward the crowd, behind the penalty box, and there they were, all these guys standing there with their bald heads/skull caps, moustaches painted on, and all kinds of signs, like OUR HERO, BEARCAT! They started parading around the arena. And I'm thinking, *Oh, my god…* Charlie, meanwhile, was just killing himself laughing.

Naturally, it got a lot of TV play.

Eventually, they had T-shirts for sale and club stationery. All kinds of stuff. I mean, it was crazy. But they were good guys. Just hockey fans, having fun. They'd send me videos of themselves from all over the place—Hawaii, some exotic island or other—horsing around, wearing all their Bearcat gear.

While this was going on, a bunch of students from the big university in Montreal, McGill, got wind of it—all kids from Calgary, going to school out East—and they started a Montreal chapter of the Bearcat Murray Fan Club. They were looking forward to seeing me, and vice-versa.

That's the one time I had the flu and couldn't make it to Montreal. They were quite disappointed. But Allan was there along with a couple of the owners—Norm Green told me later they'd scared the hell out of him—and these guys accosted them on the stairway, telling them they were the Bearcat Murray Fan Club, Montreal branch. Of course they'd had a few beers. But again, just having fun.

Next trip down there, I met with them after practice and went down to the bar on their campus and had a good time with them. They all wound up back in Calgary eventually. Smart kids, wound up being doctors and lawyers. I'd see them later, after they were in business. They'd come and see me.

So a lot of crazy stuff happened in that '86 series against Edmonton, for sure.

COLIN PATTERSON
Calgary Flames, 1983–91

People still talk about the Bearcat Murray Fan Club in Boston. I distinctly remember the first time I saw those guys, maybe four, five, or six of them.

I'm skating around during warm-up at the Garden, look up, and there they are, their skull caps with the tufts of hair sticking out the sides, fake moustaches, wearing the tracksuits just like Bearcat did. And you're thinking, *What the hell?*

The next time we went to Boston they had sweatshirts with the BEARCAT MURRAY FAN CLUB on the front, so I found out where these guys were selling them and I bought my dad one for Christmas. And he *loved* it. Best gift he received that year.

When Bearcat came out onto the ice and you were hurt, you knew you were in good hands. I had numerous injuries over the years so I dealt a lot with him.

One time I went in a corner—I should've turned, didn't see anybody coming, taking my time—got hit, and cracked my chin on the dasher. Knocked out, blood all over the place. Bearcat was out there, calling for the stretcher. I sorta woke up and he told me, "Patter, we're getting a stretcher." And I said, "No f—ing way you're getting a stretcher. Just pick me up and get me off." And he said, "Okay." It looked a lot worse than it actually was. So he got me off, stitched me up, made sure I got checked for concussion—this was long before protocol like they have today—and phoned me a couple times that night to make sure I was doing okay.

He did have this uncanny knack for drawing attention, though. We used to joke that during a nationally televised game he'd be out there like a shot, really quick, if someone got hurt. But if the game wasn't being broadcast coast-to-coast, he'd just, you know, kind of make his way out. If the game was being nationally televised, though, he'd also put his knee on your chest and tell you to stay down for a minute.

We'd beaten the Jets, a 3–0 best-of-five sweep, in the first round of playoffs that year. Then nobody, and I mean *nobody*, outside of our room gave us a chance of knocking off the Oilers…like I said, and will continue to say for as long as I live, the most memorable moment for me during my career.

I still show people those pictures I talked about, of me after Game 7 up in Edmonton, as excited as I'd ever been, going absolutely crazy, and try to explain to them, "There. That's what it's all about. That's what makes this job, makes this game, so special."

I mean, you look at the players on their team. Gretzky. Messier. Coffey. Fuhr. Kurri. Lowe. They'd won, what, two Cups in a row? They'd wind up winning, what, five in all?

Beating them at that time just seemed like a job that couldn't be done. By anyone.

But somehow we did it.

PERRY BEREZAN
Calgary Flames, 1984–89

He saved me once. This is the character of Bearcat, taking care of his guys. With him, it was always, "Don't worry, I've got your back."

One morning, I was injured and for whatever alarm malfunction, I didn't wake up in time for practice. Of course, nobody's calling to get me up because there are no cell phones in those days. I woke up at the time practice was set to start, 10:00 AM. I race to the rink. Practice is already going. I'm in a panic. The worst—worst—thing you can be is late for practice.

Bearcat sees me and says, "Get on the table! Get on the table right away! Badger's looking for you." And I'm like, *Oh, f—k. . .*

Then Bear says, "I already told him that you picked up an injury and I told you to come in later, while practice was on, so that you didn't bother anybody."

So I dive on the table and Badger comes in. "You're here! Good. Good. Bearcat told you you could be late, so it's okay."

Whether you're injured or not, being late for practice means deep s—t. The deepest.

That was the only time I was ever late for practice in all the years I played. And I've never forgotten it. Bearcat, looking out for his guys, covering my a—.

He was our psychologist, best friend, parent figure, and trainer. He was everything.

One thing I'll never, ever forget is getting home from that 45-minute charter after Game 7 against the Oilers.

I was happier than I'd ever been after a win, because of all the games, all the fights, all the times we'd lost to them in the past. And then we got home and there were 20,000 people at the airport to meet us! So many you couldn't move. Incredible, just incredible.

I had that cast on my leg, from going into the stands after Allan earlier in the series, and the crowd kept crushing in. It was mayhem. There were two little kids in the middle of it all, scared to death, bawling. Well, geez. I picked them up and carried them out, away from the crowd. I was scared they might get crushed!

The whole thing was unbelievable.

What I remember most about the next series, against St. Louis, is how damn hot it was in the old rink there, the Checkerdome. That arena was a dump. You were just sweating to death in there. It was like a sauna, literally. So Bobby and I went to the manager of the rink and told him, "We've got a helluva problem here. It's so hot. We can't stand it. We're dying. Nobody's got any air conditioners or even fans to circulate the air." And he said, "Well, I do. But don't tell anybody." So he brought these coolers in for us to use in our dressing room. He was a great guy. And the Blues didn't even know that. But it really helped us; made such a difference. Bobby and I were just ecstatic about that.

That was a really tough series against St. Louis. I mean, any team that has Brian Sutter as captain isn't going to be an easy out. A real good player, a great leader, and a fantastic person. I knew all those Sutters from the time they were snot-nosed kids, all played against us in the junior ranks and then in the NHL. Brian was one of the guys who you really hated to lose to, but you absolutely loved the man. A friend.

The fans there in St. Louis were a crazy bunch at that time. I remember Shirley coming to me after one of the games there and telling me a bunch of our people sitting in the stands, cheering for the Flames, of course, had had beer poured on them.

Going the seven games took an awful lot out of us. In the end, looking back, it probably cost us the Cup. We didn't have any time to rest or prepare for the next series.

It seemed like a rush. We were worn out.

One thing I do remember about that series is that the old Atlanta trainer, Norm Mackie—the guy who walked into the Corral, took one look, and walked out again—was there. Because he walked out, remember, I got the job as the Flames' trainer in the first place. He was sick at that time, in '86, but he was still hanging around all the time and that bothered the hell out of me because I knew he was trying to get the job back.

Then we lost to the Canadiens in the final. Big thrill, getting that far for the first time. I'll never forget the second game, at home. You always hear about momentum-shifting games in series? Well, if you're ever looking a perfect example of that, remind people of Game 2 in '86.

We'd won the first one, so we were feeling pretty good about our chances, playing again at home. Then we were ahead in Game 2 but they tied it up, so we were going to overtime. We were heading out of the dressing room to begin the overtime and I was running around trying to get things ready—took me a few minutes—and by the time I was on my way out to the bench all the guys were trooping back into the room, off the ice.

I was stunned. "What the hell happened? Can't be over yet?!" Well, it was. Faced the puck off and they scored right away, after nine seconds via future Flame Brian Skrudland.

We never really recovered after that.

As I said, it was tough to lose the series. Being so close, you never know if you'll ever get back again, but the city was absolutely ecstatic that we'd reached the Final. The franchise had never been that far before.

We were treated like kings, as if we'd won.

Shouldn't have been surprised, though. That's the kind of fans, the kind of people, we have here in Calgary.

You know, when it was over, we were all disappointed, of course, but I never sensed that anybody felt like, *Damn! We've lost our one chance...*

Everybody was pretty keen, felt that we had a good team, everything was in place; that we would get back there again and make amends.

AL MACINNIS
Calgary Flames, 1982–94

The first thing that comes to my mind about Bearcat is energy. Honestly. Am I surprised he's 88? No. Will I be surprised when he's 108? No.

The other thing that probably goes along with it is this—I don't know if the guy's ever had a bad day. In all honesty, I can't remember him having a bad day at the rink. Always working his nuts off to get guys on the ice.

Looking back, I can't ever remember him being in a bad mood or grouchy or down or sour.

I don't know what it's like in dressing rooms today, I'm not in there, but in those days, especially with Bear, he was always in the middle of everything, getting a chuckle. We were always busting his balls about tape jobs, injuries, what have you. But always in a back-and-forth good spirit. He could dish it out pretty good, too.

I don't know what it is about trainers, but they're really protective of their turf. Especially back then, they did it all. I can't think of the year but one time I was pushing for us to bring in a full-time massage therapist. That's when Bear got sensitive, right? *What the f—k do we need a full-time massage therapist for?!*

100

So he went in the back and pulled out this book—must've weighed 10 pounds—with about five inches of dust on it. *I've read this f—ing book about massage therapy! We don't need a full-time massage therapist!'* And I was trying to explain to him, "But Bear, you have so much on your plate. You can't do everything."

I don't think I convinced him but I did get a chuckle, watching him haul out this book with 40 pounds of dust on it.

Guys used to bring in doughnuts to the rink. One day, I think it was Dave Hindmarsh, brought in plain doughnuts. Bearcat was not shy. He loved the doughnuts. I don't know if you've ever seen hot wax. You soak your wrists and hands in it and let it dry, a deep-healing type of treatment. So Dave brings in these plain doughnuts one day and dipped the top of them in this wax. Well, when the wax dried it looked identical to glaze.

So he put the dozen doughnuts or whatever on the trainer's table. Like always, Bearcat comes in, we're all peeking around the corner, and he had to have been on doughnut three or four before he realized the glaze tasted funny.

101

CHAPTER 9

THE PUSH IN '89

WE'D WON THE PRESIDENTS' TROPHY for most points in the league in '88. Then again in '89.

To me, doing that meant more maybe even than winning in the playoffs. It's something Scotty Munro instilled in me way back in juniors. The best team isn't always the team that wins a championship. Winning the most games, having the most points, that's more of a real indicator of who's the best.

Well, we did that in back-to-back seasons.

It was very disappointing, losing in '88, because we were swept by the Oilers. Expectations were really high that year. But I guess it shows that sometimes you've got to be knocked down and get back up in order to realize everything it actually takes to win.

By '88–89 we'd gotten better. Remember how I talked about the great moves Cliff had made back in '86 to improve the team? Well, same thing getting Doug Gilmour for '89. When he arrived, you noticed a difference right away. Not a very big guy, as everyone knows, but just a helluva hockey player. Could make plays, score, check. Did everything. Knock him down on his a—, he'd get right back up. Wasn't intimidated by anything or anyone.

Defiant is a good to describe Killer. And he fit right in with the gang right away.

DOUG GILMOUR
Calgary Flames, 1988–92

I was in Calgary for three and a half years, and when I arrived Bear was already a legend. For me, Bearcat, AlCat, Bobby were just good guys. Salt-of-the-earth people.

Bearcat, he marketed himself the right way. Trainers don't do that. They're usually content to stay in the background. But everyone knew Bearcat. He had this larger-than-life persona. And for us players, you knew he'd be there when you needed him. He was like a teammate. We won together and we lost together and Bearcat was part of that.

Right now, with COVID-19, one of the things that's really cool, that helps you get through it, is all these classic games being on TV again; getting to relive great memories. Game 6 in Montreal in '89, for instance, and there's Bearcat on the bench, like Lanny, a lifer there, a heart-and-soul guy.

You see him and how can you not smile?

Another guy who impressed me in that way was Rob Ramage, No. 55. He did such a good job for us, especially after Suter broke his jaw in the first round against Vancouver. We'd acquired Ramage late the year before, if I remember correctly.

Killer, though, was such a funny guy, got involved with all the jokes we played. He was a leader but didn't outwardly act like one. Nothing showy. Never yelled or screamed or knocked over anything in the room.

Lanny is what you think of immediately as a leader. He had this immediate presence. Quiet, too. He'd say something when it needed to be said and all the guys would be waiting for him to speak.

But Killer, he just led by the way he played, how much he cared. Guys naturally followed his example. They figured if he's playing that hard, I darn well should, too. You can't fake that. Born that way.

We had, as I said, such a tremendous array of talent. And everyone got along so well, the way it had been in '86.

JOE NIEUWENDYK
Calgary Flames, 1986–95

Bearcat could get into the day-to-day banter with the guys. Wasn't offended by anything. Chopper (Al MacInnis) in particular loved giving Bear a hard time.

Whenever Bear would take out stitches, he'd put his bifocals on and squint. So we'd joke that since five had been put in, how come he took seven out. Chopper would get into it with him, saying, "Show me your papers. Show me your medical papers, prove you're qualified to do this job." And Bearcat would give it right back to him.

I can still see him scooting all over the ice on those spikes. He was the only trainer that had them at the time.

And one Halloween at our team party Paul Ranheim and I dressed up as Bearcat and AlCat.

He was awesome. Never in a bad mood. Back in those days it was so enjoyable to come to the rink, and having a guy like that there to greet you, with that big goofy smile or a joke, only added to that feeling. He was a guy you could hang with. Today, maybe it's more job-oriented. Back then, it was still kind of like you see in the old videos of hockey or in *Slap Shot*.

He was just one of the guys.

We'd called Theo Fleury up that year and couldn't get rid of him, he was playing so well. Just an antagonistic guy, played with a chip on his shoulder that was bigger'n he was.

He and I got along good right off the bat because I'd played hockey with his dad, Wally, in Estevan and knew him really well. A pretty good player, Wally; a little guy like me. At that time, our league, the

Allan Cup team, had folded and these guys who ran the oil company in Carlyle wanted me to come play for them. Said they'd pay me $15 a game. And Wally Fleury was my centreman.

So Theo and I had that tie when he arrived to play for the Flames. We'd always talk about his dad and his dad had told him all about me. So we hit it off, right off the bat.

THEOREN FLEURY
Calgary Flames, 1989–99

When my dad worked as a chain-spinner on the oil rigs down in Oxbow in the '60s, he played in a good senior league called the Big Six. Well, one of the first things that happened the first time I walked into the dressing room at the Saddledome was Bear coming over and telling me, "I just want you to know, I played hockey against your dad." I was like, "What?" But that gave us a connection right away. I can't imagine what kind of player Bearcat would've been. A——quick, I'm sure. Dad told me Bear was hard to play against.

A good guy. Do anything for you. Assistant coach Tom Watt used to say all the time that Bear was "like a fart in a curtain rod."

He had his favourites. The guys who rubbed him the wrong way didn't get much in the way of training services. And he was in really, really good shape. A few times he and I would wrestle each other in the dressing room. A strong guy, even at his age.

He didn't use anything in the dressing room that he wasn't getting a cut of. Then he'd promote the s—t out of whatever it was to us. Remember when that Flexall rub came out? Well, in those days Bearcat was smothered in Flexall. Head-to-toe. T-shirt, hats. You name it.

Long before all the energy drinks started coming out, Bear had his own little concoction. He called it The Okotoks. I have no idea what was in it; it tasted terrible. But it worked.

That first round of playoffs, the Canucks series…that was downright scary. It wasn't supposed to be but they pushed us to the limit.

I can still see Vernie making those saves off Stan Smyl in the overtime of Game 7. Let me tell you, those stopped my heart! Because I knew what a good player Smyl was; had seen him during his junior career with New Westminster.

Game 7 went right down to the wire, overtime. Then the puck went in off Otto's skate. Well. Sometimes you need a kick in the pants to get going.

Starting with that, everything seemed to go right for us. Deflection off a skate. Timely goal when we needed one most. Big save by Vernie when we needed one most.

Even factoring in all the bad refereeing, it seemed…meant to be for us. Just happened.

We beat L.A. and Chicago the next two series.

DOUG RISEBROUGH
Calgary Flames, 1982–87; assistant coach 1987–89; head coach 1990–91; assistant general manager 1989–90; general manager 1991–95

Bearcat had a big ego, which was a good thing. In some people it is. It pushes them to want to do more. He wanted to make a difference.

He liked people, people liked him, he loved being the centre of attention and he wanted to be somebody. Loved Calgary. Loved the Flames.

At the end of the day, it was his life, right? God forbid you called him Jim. He hated that. It was Bear or Bearcat. He, himself, was a storyline.

When you look at Bearcat's training, it was all on the job. But he persevered, always wanting to learn more. Ultimately, he gained a lot of people's confidence. We spent a lot of time together while I was playing, because I spent a lot of time in the training room.

Some guys are a good-luck charm. Bearcat was one of those guys.

Did you ever hear about his trailer down by the river? Well, he had this little trailer, got it from a farmer friend named Rockafellows, and he could pull that trailer and park it right by the Bow River and then he'd sit there with a beer, little umbrella, and fish.

Remember that night in Calgary when he raced onto the ice in the playoffs against L.A. and we scored that goal—which they ended up letting stand? I was an assistant coach that year. Well, from then on, after that dash, for the rest of the playoffs part of my job was making sure whenever one of our guys got hurt, I had to get hold of the Bearcat's pants. Because he was like a pointer dog, right? Up on that bench, one foot on the boards, straining on the leash, always ready to go.

The Chicago series is remembered for one thing: everybody still talks about Crispie climbing the glass to plant a kiss on Norma MacNeil after MacInnis scored in overtime of Game 4 at the old Stadium. Crispie's wife, Sheila, was sitting right there, next to Norma! I was standing in his line and he almost knocked me on my a— trying to go over the glass. I'm thinking, *Holy s—t, he's going into the crowd. Someone's gonna kill him.* Well, over he went, grabbed the first woman in front of him and that just happened to be Norma. Oh, geez, it was really funny and exciting but we were a bit worried, to be honest.

And thank god he found Norma. Imagine if he'd just found some random lady in the crowd. We might've had a helluva mess.

As it was, I'm sure he had a lot of explaining to do that night to Sheila.

TERRY CRISP
Calgary Flames head coach, 1987–90
The Potlicker? He wasn't only a trainer. Oh, no. He often acted an assistant coach, sometimes a head coach, too.

When I started the job in Calgary, I had a meeting with Bearcat—he was the first guy I wanted to talk to—and said, "Listen, I'm coming into this thing new. You know it better than I ever will." And I meant that.

Because, let's be honest, the bloodline for any team is its trainer. He knows more than owners, GMs, assistant GMs, or any of the coaches, whoever you want to name in any organization. I fully understood that.

What I did say to him, though, was, "I don't want a squealer. What I do want is a man who's going to do what's best for the organization, what should be done and said. I want you on *our* team but I also want you on *my* team."

You know Bearcat. "Don't you worry about me," he said. "I'll know what to tell you and what not to tell you." And I told him, "Okay, we've got a deal."

Bearcat was my go-to. It's not a slam, by any means, but the players talked around him every day. Buses, airports, planes, hotel lobbies. He's just part of the furniture, right? They don't hold back. Nobody minded because Bearcat was there.

What he brought to the job was common sense. He had the doctors and used the doctors but he also knew what to ask the doctors.

He was the King. I don't know how many times he'd come through my office door and sit down. *Okay. Lay it on me.* And he'd say, "Well, Crispie, I think you're being a little hard on so-and-so. You should lighten up a bit on this guy or that guy." Or, on the flip side, "Crispie, if I was you I'd give so-and-so a rest tonight." He knew. He had the temperature of the room.

Or if I wanted a message relayed to one or two players from the head coach, the assistant coaches, or the upper office, I'd call Bear in and tell him. And all he'd say is, "Covered."

Problem solved.

He helped get the mix I wanted. He was an old curmudgeon, had been everywhere, done everything, met everyone, knew the guys, knew the sporting world.

Oh, he could get a bit ornery from time to time. Joey Mullen had seven or eight kids—actually, three or four little boys—and they were hellions.

This was back in the good old days when kids were welcome in the room and at practice. Just turn 'em loose.

One time, Bearcat came into my office and said, "Crispie, I'm tired of being a blankety-blank-blank babysitter! Those kids, first off I see them trying to swim in the hot tub, so I had to shoo 'em out of there. Then they're in the weight room trying to lift 400 pounds. Next thing I know they're up in the top of the rink, the very top row, and I gotta go get 'em!"

He's was hot but I'm laughing.

I said, "Okay, Bear. We'll find the right way to get this calmed down." And he said, "Whatever. But that's it.

My babysitting career is *over!*"

After surviving that Vancouver scare, it seemed we just got better and better as we went along, and then, of course, we met Montreal in the Final.

Naturally, we did our share of celebrating in the aftermath of that win in Montreal in Game 6. We had the tribute the city put on at Olympic Plaza, with all the people. But I remember the night we got home and kind of stumbled off the airplane, it was daylight and we wound up going down to a bar owned by a friend of Jamie Macoun on 12th Ave. The wives, everybody, went. A wonderful visit, considering how early in the morning it was and how much a lot of us had had to drink.

Allan did a few things with the Cup. He was working at the OH Ranch west of Longview, Doc Seaman's ranch, at the time. Doc had hired him as a roustabout, a cowboy, for the off-seasons. Allan took the Cup out there and got pictures of his horse eating oats out of it. One photo went national, made it into every damn paper in the country. Or at least it seemed that way.

The best part was sharing the Cup with everybody, all of our friends. We were living in Calgary at the time, and let all the neighbours know they were welcome. Every person in Altadore showed up for pictures and things. Another time we went out to my campground on the Bow River. Those people who owned the land invited everybody in the Davisburg area, and we had a helluva shindig at their farm. My dad was still around then, so he came to a lot of these functions, which was wonderful.

Now, everybody gets to take the Cup for a day, if I'm not mistaken. There are rules. Back then, all you had to do was speak up. Allan must've hauled it here and there, all over Hell's Half Acre, 10 times.

We had so much fun just taking it over to someone's house. I must've brought the Cup here to Okotoks—must've—but I can't specifically remember doing it. You know who I know did bring it to Okotoks? Hall of Famer Bert Olmstead. He'd won the Cup five times of course, during his playing days in Montreal and Toronto. He lived around here in those days, in Black Diamond.

My friends, the people who'd been with me through my various careers—on the rigs, jockeying, all that—they probably thought having the Cup here was more special than I did. I mean, they'd see it and their eyes would light up, like Christmas morning. They'd be there, snapping pictures, so excited. Special people, good friends. Shirley and I felt great about being able to share the Cup with them.

I mean, nothing too crazy, really. But it was obviously very, very enjoyable. And, honestly, we thought we'd get more practice at it; doing the whole thing again and again.

CHAPTER 10

THE FALL

AFTER WE WON THE STANLEY CUP IN 1989, it sure looked as if we'd win a few more. We certainly had the team, the players, to do that.

But for different reasons, we kept losing guys, important guys. First Lanny retired, and Pepper, Jim Peplinski, just up and quit. That kind of started the whole thing. Hakan Loob went back to Sweden.

We lost the series to L.A. in '90, then Crispie was fired. Cliff Fletcher left and went to Toronto the year after that.

Doug Gilmour. Al MacInnis. Joel Otto. Joe Mullen. Brad McCrimmon. The list goes on and on. One after the other.

Even a guy like Rob Ramage, who'd played so well for us the spring we won. He might not have gotten the attention he deserved, but he did a helluva job in that run. But you turned around and, *poof!*, he was gone too.

People talk about the money and the part it played in the breakup, but I didn't get into that, obviously. What bothered me, still does to this day, is the constant disrupting of that team.

I thought we should've won a few before '89, being honest with you—in '86, '87, '88, we were good enough those years too. We just couldn't win with Badger Bob.

So we hired Crispie, finally got 'er done, then only a few years later, you couldn't recognize the group, so much had changed. The karma, the feeling, or whatever you want to call it had, was gone. So many of the old guys had left and new guys came in and…well, it just wasn't the same.

We were beaten in Game 6 at L.A. in 1990. We had a perfectly good goal by Gilmour called off in overtime. No replay then. Denis Morel was the ref, of course. That would've sent the series back home for a deciding game. No doubt in my mind we would've won that and then, who knows?

But no use crying over spilled milk. What's done is done.

Losing Killer really, really hurt. I remember after we'd made that big trade with Toronto, Cliff had taken all our guys, five of 'em, including Gilmour. Anyway, he was sitting up in the stands at Maple Leaf Gardens one time we were in there to play, and I wandered up to say hello.

"Hi, Cliff. Howya doing?"

"Fine, Bear. How about you?"

"Okay. But I'm sure pissed at you. In fact, I'm madder'n a SOB."

"Why?"

"You stole all our players. How could you do that to us?"

"Geezus, Bear." He gritted his teeth. "I *had* to do it. Just trying to make my team better. How in hell could I not make that trade if I had the chance? I don't know why I'm explaining it to you anyways."

And I said, "Well, I wanted to let you know because I love you."

I think he got a kick out of that. But you look back at that deal—we lost five guys, main guys. Gilmour, Jamie Macoun, Ric Nattress, and Rick Wamsley off the Cup team.

We picked up that hotshot guy from Toronto, Gary Leeman, then he ends up wanting to sue us because he says he was injured, got hurt in a game. Like hell he was.

Oh, it was bad.

That team had been carefully built, had everything you could want. I mean, we could play any way you wanted. Tough game, we were fine. Skating game, same. Really good players, up and down the lineup.

Everyone got along great.

Everything seemed to be tickity-boo.

But we lost that series to L.A. the next year and, as I said, everything started to change. For a long time, we had this replica Stanley Cup, full-size top-to-bottom but cut in half, up on the wall in the dressing room, hanging kinda cockeyed, with everybody's names from the '89 team on it.

Well, one day—for the life of me I can't remember what year it was—Stewie, a great guy who worked in the dressing room with us, he came over, really quiet, and told me, almost in a whisper, "Jimmy. Jimmy. Jimmy. We've got a problem." They'd thrown this half-a-Cup in the dumpster out back of the Saddledome. This was in the middle of the night.

I mean, I could understand in a way, because we weren't a very good team at the time.

So I said to Stewie, "Where is it?" He told me and then warned, "They're getting ready to take it tonight, to the dump."

Well, geez.

So I went out back and climbed into that damn dumpster. I'm down on my hands and knees, in the dark, crawling around. This thing was full of garbage. Found it right at the far end, though, kinda dented up and marked up 'cause it had been bounced around. So I rescued it.

I kept it in the dressing room for a little while and thought, *Well, geez, I better get it out of here. There's a reason they were throwing it away.* So I brought it home.

And I half-a— kinda forgot about it. It just sat there, in my basement, for years and years and years. Then, in September 2020, a group of the guys from '89 were coming over here, Colin Patterson, a bunch of them. Before they visited, I said to Patter, "Ask the guys if they want this. The alumni should have this. But what can you do with it, how best to save it?"

They said, "We'll put 'er on the wall in that bar in the Saddledome, above the press box."

"Well," I said, "that's a helluva deal."

So when they came out here and I showed them this half-a-Cup, they were just thrilled. Like little kids. It brought back such great memories of that whole run.

Lanny was here, everybody. And I told them the whole story.

I'm only glad it's found a home again.

CHAPTER 11

TRICK OF THE TRADE

I'M OFTEN ASKED ABOUT THE SPIKED SHOES I used to wear and how they came to be.

Well, when I worked for the Centennials I was having so much trouble, sliding around when I needed to get out on the ice quickly to help an injured player. Just a real pain.

Oh, I tried all kinds of things. When I was working with the CFL Stampeders, they came up with knobby-type shoe bottoms for that new kind of turf they had. Well, those turned out to be dangerous.

Next I gave those broom ball shoes with foam, really thick rubber soles, a try. They worked pretty good, but they'd come apart like a two-dollar watch when I was walking around the area on the cement. They didn't last. So I scratched them off the list.

I had a friend who was a trainer with Winnipeg in World Hockey, in the Bobby Hull days. Well, he tried wearing golf shoes. I did, too, but they were too damned slippery; they wouldn't dig in. So then I had an idea. I took them to my skate sharpener and sharpened the spikes so they had a point on 'em instead of a flat spike. They worked a lot better but I still wasn't satisfied.

There had to be something better.

Every time we were down in the states on a road trip and had time off, I'd wander into the stores, in search of something better that I might be able to use. I'd thought of indoor track shoes. I took my problem to my shoemaker, Tony Poscente—he owned Tony's, a shoe shop on 16th Avenue and Centre Street. Now it's a hot dog stand or something.

Tony tried like hell to find the spikes for the indoor track shoes, but he couldn't because they were all European made. We could get the nut-part that went into the shoe but not the spikes, the little short ones.

Well, gall darn.

We used to buy a lot of equipment through Tony, too, beginning in juniors with the Centennials. He was a friend of Scotty Munro's. Tony had a wonderful wife, a Ukrainian lady. So she got me talking Ukie, Tony got me talking Italian, and we became great friends. He'd repair stuff and we ended up buying—this is with Bobby and the Flames now—nearly everything through him. Sticks. Elbow pads. Shin pads. All he did was bill us. He took care of everything. I told Bobby, "Just leave it to Tony." Bobby ended up loving him, too.

But back to the spikes in my shoes...

One time we were in L.A., I was out shopping, and I walked by a big, open table, like a pool table with a big sign: EVERYTHING FOR SALE. They had all kinds of stuff on there. It was piled high, overflowing onto the floor.

Anyway, I was just a little bit past the table and out of the corner of my eye I spotted something, stopped, didn't even turn around, just backed up. And there, sticking out of a pile of stuff was one of those long track spikes. They had to be four or five inches long. I went digging in there and pulled out these shoes. Well, they had to be a size 15 or 16. I got looking at them, and *bingo!*, went up to the till and asked how much they were—$2 or something. The cashier girl looked at these huge shoes and little me and asked, "Are those for *you*?!"

She started laughing so I explained the whole story.

I thought I'd just take the spikes out, take the shoes to Tony, he'd tear the shoes apart, pull those nuts out, and put 'em in my running shoes. Pretty smart, eh? And that's exactly what we did. Tony inserted in a really short spike, a high-jump spike he called 'em, that just barely stuck out from the sole. But they gripped that ice like a damn and they weren't damaged walking around anywhere else in the rink.

I never had a problem again.

Do you know, I couldn't interest any of my fellow trainers in the value of the shoes. They were amazingly helpful. Not only for the athlete laying on the ice, but for yourself. They really, really helped me get around out there safely.

I ended up finding some in Texas that were like toe rubbers but had those little spikes—more like rivets—in them. I bought a half-dozen of those for the hell of it and brought 'em home.

At the time, I'd hired an ambulance to be at all of our home games strictly for us, to not bother with anything that might happen up in the crowd because the city ambulance was there primarily to take control if somebody in the stands had a heart attack or needed assistance quickly. We needed help specifically for our players. I mean, what happens if the paramedics were up in the crowd administering to somebody and then I needed them for something potentially dangerous on the ice?

So I took these rubber shoes and gave them to the ambulance outfit that I'd hired. The guy who owned the company was named Sigurdson. He was from Cochrane and also worked the Calgary Stampeders football games.

I told him, "The first thing you do when you'd drive into the rink is put these rubber shoes on. I want you to have them on even during warm-up because if I need you, I need you now. I don't need you slipping on your a—." Well, those ambulance personnel, they fell in love with those things.

Sigurdson's son is now an Alberta MP for the Conservative Party. We got to be good friends. He'd help me with first-responder work, the kind of things you need to know at the scene of a wreck, and I taught them how to tape people up if they were out on the road and injured before getting them into ambulance and off to the hospital.

He told me, "Bear, those shoes you gave us are more valuable to us out on black ice than on your hockey ice, if there's a wreck on the road and we're trying to pull people around. They're *awesome*!"

That's basically how it started and how valuable they were.

MARK DEPASQUALE
Calgary Flames equipment manager, 2006 to present

I was a young guy working the visiting locker room in Chicago back during the 1989 playoffs and the Flames came to town.

Something happened on the ice—can't remember what, exactly, who got hurt—and I look up to see this crazy guy, going full speed across the ice. At the old Stadium you had to walk across the ice to get to the bench, so I knew how slippery it was.

When I'd bring a buddy or two of mine to fill in, they always fell and the crowd would go wild. Anyway, I thought, *Look at this son of a gun, sprinting!*

I thought he was crazy.

"I did help Bearcat bring somebody who had been hurt down the stairs at the old Chicago Stadium. He came down all 20-something steps after the period—you had to walk down steps to get to the dressing rooms at the old building—and I could hear the clicking.

Click! Click! Click!

I knew he had some kind of spikes on his shoes. That stuck with me. So did the grin on his face. The laughing with his players is still, all these years later, unforgettable.

CHAPTER 12

BEHIND THE CURTAIN

THE FALL AFTER WE WON THE CUP, the whole team went over to the Soviet Union and the Czech Republic to represent the league in a bunch of exhibition games. A couple of those were played in Prague and four more in the USSR, the last one against Red Army, the big club.

That was 1989, remember, and nothing had changed in those countries yet. So the experience would be unique. Some people were convinced that we'd have all kinds of problems, but personally I found it quite easy working there. I think Bobby felt the same way. The language thing cropped up from time to time, but we had translators assigned to us all the time, taking care of us. We didn't have trainer-specific help or anything, but we got along really well and managed to get what we needed.

I had one problem, though. I like vodka, but I prefer it with orange juice. Well, when they brought out the vodka in Russia, I got real excited because this is the genuine article. But when I asked for orange juice they were p—ed right off. As if I'd offended them. They said, "No! *Nyet!* You don't drink anything with vodka!" Straight-up. No mix. And that's the way they made us drink it. I actually got a kick out of that.

Other than that, they kept us out of trouble with the black-market guys. I brought lots of stuff back, mostly crystal from Czech. We even had a deal with a store and the government where they brought all the inventory right to the hotel for us! And then they flew them back to Canada for us. We just had to go pick everything up at customs.

It was an absolutely tremendous experience for all of us, because Shirley came along and so did both of my boys. Allan was going anyway as an assistant trainer, and Danny came along too.

From a competitive standpoint, we really were at a real disadvantage. For us, that tour was our training camp, none of the players were in seasonal shape, and these teams we played, they'd been waiting for us, preparing for us. This, playing against the Stanley Cup champions, was a very big deal to them, and we were on their turf.

That certainly had to be frustrating for our players. But the way I saw it, we were so lucky to be there in the first place.

Neat story about the Russians—in 1988, at the Winter Olympics in Calgary, their figure-skating team lived and trained in Okotoks. At that time, they'd just built the new arena down there and called it the Murray Arena, honouring my family, mostly my mom and dad for all the service they'd done for the community. But also my sister and my two young brothers, Donald and Norman.

Funny thing was, the night the arena opened in 1986, with a bunch of hoopla and everything, happened to be the same night I was up in Edmonton playing against the Oilers in Game 7 of that series we won, the night I went into the stands after Allan and wrecked my leg! Yup. Same night, believe it or not. They made an announcement over the loudspeaker at the arena opening—"Bearcat Murray's broke his leg and he's in the hospital."

Anyway, back to '88 and the Olympics. My dad, he'd go down to the arena every day to watch the Russian skaters train, became good friends with all of those people. They treated him great. He had a helluva time. So the next year we were over there in Russia to play these exhibitions and they'd introduce everybody—coaches, players, us, everybody—before each game. Well, before the first game they did the introductions—Gary Roberts, Joe Nieuwendyk, Al Macinnis, Mike Vernon, and the rest of the players. All these great players who everybody in the stands knows. Well, right at the end they introduced the rest of us and when they announced me—"This is trainer Bearcat Murray, from Okotoks, Alberta"—I got this huge standing ovation from the crowd. Bigger than any of the players! I was thinking, *What is this?* The players were all shaking their heads, mouths open. They couldn't believe it. Matter of fact, neither could I!

Well, it finally dawned on me—Murray Arena, Okotoks. They recognized my name from all the coverage of the Olympic figure skating the year before! *Boom*! And they started cheering like crazy.

I'm not sure anybody else knew what in the hell was going on, but it sure did make me feel good.

CHAPTER 13

STEPPING AWAY

WHEN I RETIRED IN AUGUST OF 1996, I didn't know I was going.

The way it happened was that Al Coates—Coatesy, the general manager at the time—approached me and explained the organization was thinking about naming a Flames ambassador and that the owners wanted me to take the job. They all thought I'd be perfect for it.

Coatesy said, "You've being doing that job for years, anyway, out in the community, meeting people, along with the trainer's job, and have had a great success of it."

He told me I could stay and train until I dropped dead for all he cared; they had no problem with that. But the owners felt I'd be great in the other role, promoting the team.

Well, I was 63 and had been a trainer for the last 30 years of my life. I loved being around the guys. I know I could've done it for a couple more years; I was still in good shape and everything.

Did I feel as if I was being pushed? Yeah, sort of. I know for sure that Dave King had tried to get rid of me. He got rid of my son, Allan. *Boom*! Didn't tell him anything; they just didn't re-up his contract. King wanted his people in there. That happens a lot in pro sports, I realize, but it still doesn't make it easier to accept.

So I kinda figured something might be up. But when it happened it broke my heart. Under the circumstances, though, I thought the organization handled the whole thing pretty well. Thank god for Coatesy.

When he approached me initially, he told me to take all the time I needed to make a decision and then give them an answer. Well, I actually didn't have a lot of time because this was July, training camp wasn't far away, and the kids, the draft picks, were coming in during Stampede to work out and go through some training sessions to figure out what they had to work on, what was going to be expected of them.

I was thinking about the changeover when I drove with Doug Barkley up to Red Deer for the annual Sutter brothers golf tournament—we'd been going, Bark and I, since they started that tournament in Lethbridge. I did my thing there in Red Deer for three or four days and after I finished my auction duties the final day I got to talking with Brian Sutter, a favourite of mine. We chatted about how he didn't have a coaching job at the time. And he said, "You know Bear, I'm not worried about it. I get calls every day wanting me to coach. Phone's ringing off the hook. But I'm not going just anywhere. I'm going to go somewhere I want to be. I want this to feel right."

So I told him good luck, jumped in the car, and started driving south, out of Red Deer. That's when I made up my mind to retire and take the other job I'd been offered. I stopped the car on the shoulder of the highway, on that big hill—trucks are always parked there—and had a little cry.

I found a place and called Shirley and told her I'd made up my mind. She said, "If you're sure. Everything'll be fine. You're still getting paid." Then she let me know that it had just come over the radio that the Flames had fired Coach Pierre Page. I said, "You're kidding me?!"

So I told her I'd get right back to her, then I immediately called Brian, still partying like hell at the hotel. I told him what had happened and gave him Coatesy's number. I'd known the Sutters my whole life. And I'd have to say of all of 'em, Brian is my favourite. A great guy. Crazy. So much fun. I knew him since he first started playing junior hockey in Lethbridge, when I was with the Centennials. We'd come off the ice, same bloody walkway, he'd hit me on the a— with his stick, put his arm around me, and say, "Bearcat, ya little SOB, when are ya gonna come work for us?"

Then, as I said, I started going to the family golf tournament, their folks were always around—wonderful, wonderful people—and it went from there. I just fell in love with that family, from day one. Shirley fell in love with Mrs. Sutter. Viking, where they're from, is really close to Killam, the town my dad grew up in. So we have that connection too.

The oldest of the brothers, Gary, never played in the league. He was always down on the farm, but he was a good guy and a good hockey player. He actually worked with Allan while they were both with the Wranglers. Gary Sutter did a little bit of coaching there. They're great friends, even today.

Anyway, I knew Brian would be interested in the job, being close to home, all that. So he phoned Coatesy and wound up being hired. The perfect choice, in my opinion.

BRIAN SUTTER
Calgary Flames coach, 1997–2000; friend

Bear and I go back a long ways together, to junior days, opponents for years and years and always best friends. I remember one time playing for St. Louis in Calgary and going down. All of a sudden, there's Bearcat. I got up quick—injuries were nothing new to me—but he was like, "Brian! Brian! Ya all right?" I had to pat him on the a— right then and there, because he cared about all players, not just his own, and I made a point of thanking him later. That's how we remember him, running on the ice to help somebody with that towel going. The memory always brings a smile to my face.

Has there ever been a time *without* Bearcat? I mean, his name was synonymous with junior hockey in Calgary, along with Scotty Munro.

People tend to forget about those days. So it was special, and entirely fitting, that when the city finally got a WHA team and then an NHL team, he'd be involved. Always somebody you looked up to. I used to go the rink early during my days in St. Louis, helping trainers unpack the equipment, meaning you got to know a lot of the trainers around the league really, really well. And their families. Guys like Tommy Woodcock, Jim Pickard, Norm Mackie. Great individuals. That's the way it was with Bear. Shirley, too. She's an incredible lady to have lived with that gentleman as long as she has. And she still manages to do it with a grin on her face.

Trainers are such important parts of any team. People don't realize. The doctors had final say, of course, but you always, always trusted what the trainers had to tell you regarding injuries. Guys like Bear had the ultimate respect. Didn't hurt that people just naturally enjoyed being around him, too.

Unfortunately, when I did go to Calgary to coach he'd already retired. Having been against him for so many years, I'd have dearly loved to have worked with him. But he was still around, and that picked up everybody's spirits. Just a special, special man. All the accolades, the respect, he's earned. Honest. Told you what he thought. Nothing phoney about Bear. He was always himself. Which is as high a compliment as you can pay anyone, I think.

Bearcat Murray: Man. Myth. Legend. Potlicker.

Between learning about the coaching vacancy, telling Brian about it, and making my decision about the new job, it turned out to be quite the drive home.

Did I miss the training? Of course. Missed it right away. Being around the guys, mostly, Still do miss it, in different ways.

But I'm sure the management had a lot of meetings over my leaving that job. It wasn't an easy thing for them to bring up, to consider, and that at least made me feel good.

If you look around the league, it was kind of an occupational hazard: all the trainers were constantly scared to death for their jobs. Whenever a new coach or a manager would get hired, there was the chance they would want to bring in their own people, right? And we were such a tight-knit group, the trainers, always ready to help each other out whenever possible. A big family, everybody doing their best to make sure players—all players, not just the ones on your team—were healthy and ready to play. So it was tough, really tough, to see a guy, any guy, go. And this happened every year.

Bobby Stewart and I used to sit and talk about how lucky we were to have Cliff as our boss for so long. He stuck up for us, and I'm sure there were many times he overruled someone, allowing us to keep our jobs. Cliff protected us like crazy because he trusted us. We knew that and were grateful to him.

Anyway, by the time I got home from Red Deer and the Sutter golf tournament I'd already in my mind moved on to this new job. I enjoyed people. They just wanted to hear stories about Lanny McDonald, other guys, and I had a million of those to tell. One story just led to another to another and on and on. You know, looking back, I was busy right away in that new job and that sure helped me transition out of training and being down at the rink, at practice, every day.

Straight off I went out and hired Jungle Jim Hunter, the retired skier, one of the Crazy Canucks, to give me a public speaking course. He'd just gotten involved in that business. He was very good for me. I really went to school with him.

One time early on he told me, "Bear, I don't want you to think I'm pushing things here or giving you a tough time, but my job is to let the Bear out of the cage."

His exact words—let the Bear out of the cage.

By that, he meant he wanted more of my personality to show when I was speaking to a group. I had the stories, what people wanted to hear, but I had to learn how to tell 'em better and get my personality across.

139

I'd taken some public speaking courses before, from the Dale Carnegie outfit in Saskatchewan, but I wasn't really happy with those.

Jungle Jim Hunter said, "I've gotta teach you to open up. You're too reserved right now to be a speaker, to be doing these things. You're a nice guy and everybody loves you but I've got to get to that Bear inside you and let him out."

Well, he did.

One time early on, I remember doing a graduation speech for Western Canada High School. This was at the Jubilee Auditorium, and it was jammed full of schoolkids and parents.

This lady who was a member at Calgary Golf and Country Club asked me to do it and told me I only had two or three minutes. I told her, "Well, I can't even say my name in that short a time." Anyway, I started studying books and tapes on public speaking from famous people, through Jungle Jim, and I copied 'em. I ended up using a lot of their tricks.

At this graduation, I did this demonstration using a $10 bill in my hand to show the kids how important their life is and nothing will ever change that; that whatever happens, they'll never lose their worth, they'll always have value.

So I showed the $10 to 'em, scrunched it up in my hand, threw it on the floor, stomped on it, picked it up, and examined it. Then I folded it out, flattened it. And then I told them: "You—every one of you—is like this $10 bill here. It's been through some tough times just now, but it still maintains its value. And so will you. No matter what you go through. Never forget that."

Well, I finished—it was a helluva lot longer than two or three minutes—and the reaction...I got a standing ovation, from the parents and the students. I've got to tell you, I was speechless. Then the kids came up to get their diplomas and I made sure I kept track of each of their names in the 10 seconds or so after they were announced so when I shook hands I could say, "Way to go, Bill, and good luck in the future" or "Good job, Joanne, and good luck in the future."

I'll always remember this one little girl, she must've been the 100th to graduate or something like that, came up, and I said, "Okay, Alice, congratulations," etc. Well, she put her arms around me, gave me a hug, and said, "You're the funniest guy I've ever known!" Then she walked away.

That was so sweet, put such confidence in me. Right then and there I knew I'd be okay with this public speaking thing.

BRIAN PATAFIE
Calgary Flames training staff, 1996–98

After spending the previous two years with the Montreal Canadiens AHL training staff in Halifax, Nova Scotia, I found myself out of work because the Canadiens were moving their farm club to Sherbrooke, Quebec, and were looking for someone bilingual to fill that position.

A series of phone calls between Al Coates, Cliff Fletcher, and myself landed me the position with the Flames' farm club that was moving into Moncton, New Brunswick, just a few hours down the road from Halifax.

Arriving in Calgary for the first time ever in September of 1984 to attend the Flames' training camp, I was picked up at the airport by Bobby Stewart, and he informed me that Bearcat wanted to meet me before I'd be dropped at the Palliser Hotel.

I asked Bobby what Bearcat's real name was. He looked at me and said, "That's a great question. Nobody's ever asked that."

Arriving at the Saddledome, we went straight to the Flames' dressing room and there he was. To me, a young trainer just starting out, he looked larger than life. I nervously extended my hand and said, "Hello, Mr. Murray. I'm Brian Patafie, the trainer from Moncton."

Bearcat glanced around to see who I was talking to, then looked at me with that s—t-eatin' grin of his and said, "Hello, ya little potlicker. How was the flight?"

During the next 45 minutes that he and Bobby showed me around I was honestly totally confused because I didn't know if being called a potlicker was a good thing or a bad thing. Over the next 15 years, I came to learn that if he called you a potlicker, he liked you.

In 1996, Al Coates called again, this time informing me that Bearcat was moving upstairs and I was being brought in from Saint John to join the club's training staff.

By then, I had seen firsthand how Bearcat had almost reached deity status across southern Alberta. Meaning I was extremely hesitant to ever say I was the guy who'd be "replacing" Bearcat. No worries on that score. I was only joining the training staff. Nobody could replace what Bearcat had brought to the table.

Chapter 14

Rivals/Friends

ONE OF MY MOST CHERISHED MEMENTOS is a photo, beautifully framed, of me with Wayne Gretzky, Mark Messier, and Paul Coffey.

Barrie Stafford, the Oilers equipment manager, and Kenny Lowe, the trainer, set everything up. And I thank them for that.

As I've already mentioned, I always got along great with the Oilers. People from Calgary who were around when the rivalry was really cooking might see this particular picture—me and those three guys—and fall over in a dead faint. But that's the way it was. My younger brother, Norman, used to work with Glen Sather, when they were lifeguards in the hot pool in Banff. There were really good friends. So there were all kinds of connections.

I was already retired by the time of this photo with the three Oilers. An NHL All-Star team was in Calgary to play…the Russians, I think. Anyway, Ken and Barrie hunted me down and said, "Bear, we've always kidded around about getting a photo taken but this is a great chance to finally get 'er done. And the boys—the players—want it. No time like the present!"

All of a sudden, they took me into the dressing room and Paul Coffey grabbed me by the shoulders, kind of roughing me up. "Come on, you little potlicker! We've got to get this picture!" Then Gretzky walked in and he started hollering, "I want in! Hang you, on guys!" Then Messier showed up.

You coulda knocked me over with a feather.

We had a good time. Barrie, the instigator, took a look at us all lined up together, posing for the camera, and said, "Four Hall of Famers, right there." Barrie later sent me the photo, framed and everything.

And, well, all four of us did make it into the Hall of Fame. So I'm quite proud of that photo.

But that's the way they were all the time up in Edmonton. Wonderful people. Most of the coaches there could sound a little arrogant. They were catered to because they were tops on the totem pole in those years. For a reason. Most of the players had this superior kind of attitude—confident, I guess they might say; cocky, others might say—but they were damn good at what they did.

I'm repeating myself here, but we may have been real rivals, and the games got out of hand on a lot of nights, but I never had a problem with 'em.

I vividly remember the one time Kevin Lowe was taken down, had really been crunched, behind their net, at the Saddledome. I was standing on the bench, saw it happen. I used to give a lot of those Oilers players s—t for wearing that Gretzky helmet—actually a Jofa, but I called it a Gretzky helmet. They were terrible. What a piece of crap. Tissue-thin. A rolled-up newspaper would've given a guy more protection!

Anyway, Kevin was wearing one. He got hit, he's groggy. I instinctively jumped on the ice because he looked to be in bad shape and I got to him first. I said, "Kevin, it's Bearcat. Peter Millar is busy now so I'm out here looking after you. Everything's fine." Giving him the talk. He'd finally started coming around, Peter showed up, everything looked okay, but I scolded Kevin as he was going off the ice: "Kevin, I gotta tell you, again, you've married a very, very nice lady (former Canadian Olympic skier Karen Percy) and you've just had a baby. You're now a father, so it's about time you started worrying about them and not your own f—ing head. Get rid of that frigging crappy little helmet."

An impossibly young
Jim Murray with his best
pal, Mickey.

Bearcat and Shirley
at the start of their
journey together.

And babies make four—the
family together. Bearcat, Shirley
holding baby Danny, and Allan.

Local cartoon of the WHA Calgary Cowboys' jack-of-all-trades.

The ever-elusive goal-scoring star of the Estevan Miners.

An admirer borrowing Wayne Gretzky's first car for a spin, outside the Calgary Centennials' offices.

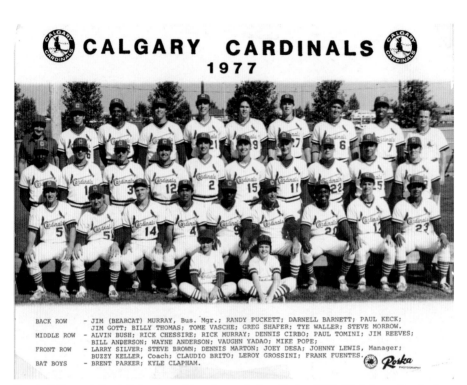

CALGARY CARDINALS
1977

BACK ROW   - JIM (BEARCAT) MURRAY, Bus. Mgr.; RANDY PUCKETT; DARNELL BARNETT; PAUL KECK;
              JIM GOTT; BILLY THOMAS; TOME VASCHE; GREG SHAFER; TYE WALLER; STEVE MORROW.
MIDDLE ROW - ALVIN BUSH; RICK CHESSIRE; RICK MURRAY; DENNIS CIRBO; PAUL TOMINI; JIM REEVES;
              BILL ANDERSON; WAYNE ANDERSON; VAUGHN YADAO; MIKE POPE;
FRONT ROW   - LARRY SILVER; STEVE BROWN; DENNIS MARTON; JOEY DESA; JOHNNY LEWIS, Manager;
              BUZZY KELLER, Coach; CLAUDIO BRITO; LEROY GROSSINI; FRANK FUENTES.
BAT BOYS   - BRENT PARKER; KYLE CLAPHAM.

Roska
PHOTOGRAPHY

Baseball Bearcat (far left, back row) in a team photo with the 1977–78 Calgary Cardinals.

Helping tend to the aches and pains of rodeo cowboys, Bearcat (far left, front row), in this instance the Calgary Stampede 1979 Alberta Team.

3

Bearcat settling into his first office at the brand-new Olympic Saddledome.

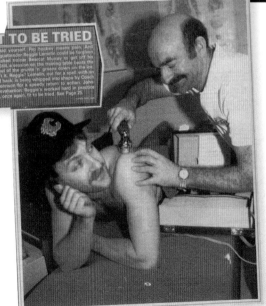

FIT TO BE TRIED

Don't kid yourself. Pro hockey means pain. And Flame goaltender Reggie Lemelin could be forgiven if he asked trainer Bearcat Murray to get off his back. Still, a session on the training table beats the heck out of the grunts 'n' groans down on the ice, doesn't it, Reggie? Lemelin, out for a spell with an injured back, is being whipped into shape by Coach Bob Johnson for a speedy return to action. Johnson's evaluation: Reggie's worked hard in practice and is, once again, fit to be tried. See Page 25.

Always a media favourite, Bearcat poses with goaltender Reggie Lemelin for the papers.

4

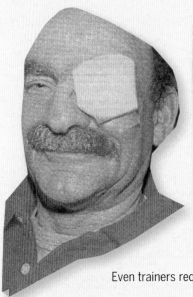

More than bloody nose

(Herald writer)

BUFFALO — A bloody nose would have been acceptable — even appreciated.

For Calgary Flames' trainer Jim (Bearcat) Murray, what appeared to be a bloody nose from a freak puck deflection Saturday night at Bloomington, Minn. is worse.

When a clearing attempt by Minnesota North Stars' Curt Giles deflected off the stick of Gary Roberts and whipped into the Flames' bench, Murray was struck by the puck just below the left eye.

"I didn't even see it coming — I was leaning over to give a player a water bottle," said a shaken Murray, his left eye heavily bandaged on the flight to Buffalo. "I just fell. I was in shock."

"You could really hear it on the bench," said Theoren Fleury.

Added Hakan Loob: "I was on the ice . . . even I could hear it."

With a towel over his nose and cheek, Murray was taken to hospital. He received 14 stitches to close the gash. He went to a hospital here on Sunday, hopeful X-rays would determine there isn't any serious damage to his left eye.

There had been too much blood buildup in it Saturday to make a proper diagnosis.

Murray also suffered a fractured left cheekbone.

He was to return to Calgary today.

Even trainers require patching up every so often.

Mr. Magic receives profile treatment in the *Calgary Sun*.

Fishing at McKinnon Flats, known to some now as Bearcat Flats, on the Bow River.

Shirley (left) and the Bear with longtime friends Jim and Joan Wilson at McKinnon Flats.

Posing with three friendly enemies from three hours north up Highway No. 2: Mark Messier, Wayne Gretzky, and Paul Coffey.

Bearcat and the Clarence Campbell Bowl, after the Flames had beaten St. Louis to reach their first Stanley Cup Final, spring 1986.

Bearcat checking out his refurbished, reconfigured Saddledome digs following dressing-room renovation.

Joe Nieuwendyk helps the ever-alert Bear get to where he needs to be.

Tending to an injured Mike Bullard.

The long-ago jockey readying for another ride in the Calgary Stampede parade.

Lanny McDonald

Bearcat Murray

Jim Peplinski

Lanny McDonald, the ol' Potlicker,
and Jim Peplinski gracing the
cover of a Flames game program.

The ol' Potlicker, as
famous a face as any of
the players under his care.

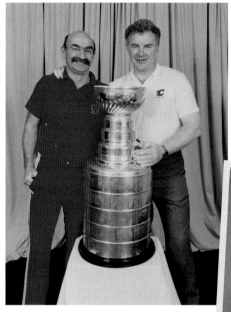

A surprise visit from the Cup to Danny Murray's 25th birthday, arranged by brother Allan. Family friend Barb Buick is on the left.

The by-now legendary trainer and head coach Terry Crisp pose alongside the Stanley Cup, 1989.

Colin Patterson, Allan Murray, Bear, and Jamie Macoun attend one of the many post-Cup win celebrations.

Danny Murray and the original Bearcat
take a turn with Lord Stanley's
hallowed silver mug.

The Murray family, including
grandad Allan, along with the object
of everyone's attention in 1989.

The Murray family together in the Soviet Union for the Flames' Friendship Tour exhibition schedule in the fall of 1989.

Bearcat is profiled in the *Calgary Herald*.

Referee Kerry Fraser waits for Bearcat to tend to shaken goaltender Rick Wamsley. Sergei Makarov (42) looks on.

Danny Murray and his dad enjoy some fly-fishing time together.

Indicating a hole-in-one at Banff Springs Golf Club during Kevin Lowe's annual charity tournament. Bob Hope would later compliment Bearcat on the achievement.

Bearcat and Shirley celebrate his induction into the Hockey Hall of Fame, 2008.

Father and son, Bear and Danny, at the 'Cat's induction into the Alberta Sports Hall of Fame, Red Deer, Alberta, 2015.

Alberta Sports
Hall of Fame & Museum

Honoured Members
Gallery

Interactives

Museum Exhibits

Later on, I ran into Kenny Lowe, Kevin's brother, and he thanked me. He told me, "Bear, it worked. You gave Kevin hell about that helmet. And he listened. He finally threw that SOB away! I've been trying to get him to do that for a long time."

It shows you, though, that there was a certain trust between the two sides. Kevin was also one guy I had confidence that I could tell that to. He understood that I had his best interests—all their best interests—at heart. And vice-versa. I mean, I never would have said that to Gretzky. But Kevin I could talk to. He'd listen.

And, you gotta understand, I probably participated in three or four golf tournaments every summer with those guys. And we'd goof around together. They'd treat me as if I was a brother; were just awesome to me. So much fun. Matter of fact, my only hole-in-one came at an Oilers golf tournament, Kevin Lowe's tournament, at Banff Springs! We were on Hole No. 4, called the Devil's Cauldron, at the old course. Famous, famous hole. One of my partners was a local doctor, a lady, but she wasn't there when were supposed to tee off. Shotgun start. And they wanted to get going.

Finally, Craig Simpson, the guy who's always on TV now, started yelling at me, "C'mon Bear, we've got to get a move on! Hit the ball!" So I grabbed my club, a 6-iron, raced up to the tee box, and he said, "Go!"

Well, I hit the gall-darned thing and as it was in the air, Simpson, real excited, was yelling, "Bear! It's in! It's in the hole!" Ball hit the green, bounced three or four times, and rolled right in. *Bingo!* Great shot. A real humdinger. Well, everybody was going nuts.

Later, when I ran into Kevin, probably back up at the clubhouse, he was pretty ticked-off, almost apologetic. I asked him why. Geez, I was happier'n hell. He said, "Bear, I'm so mad. I wanted the hole-in-one car to be on that hole. On No. 4. And they put it on another hole instead."

So I would've won a car! Oh, well.

The one other crazy thing about that crazy day? There was a VIP playing the course at the same time as the tournament and we had to

wait for him all the time, stay out of his way. The weather was bad but he was still out there, playing, by himself, except for the woman who drove the cart.

You'll never guess.

Bob Hope.

They'd let him on the course because, well, he's Bob Hope.

Later on, Ol' Ski Nose actually took the time to come over and shake my hand. "You're the guy with the hole-in-one, right?" he said to me. "Way to go. I've had a hole-in-one myself."

How great is that?

And if that wasn't enough, a guy, a fireman here in town who was also a painter, later presented me with a canvas of that hole, the Devil's Cauldron, looking from the tee box out toward the green. That painting was better than getting a trophy or an award. It's still one my most prized possessions.

So as you can see, I had a lot of great times being around the Edmonton Oilers. Despite the rivalry.

KEN LOWE
Edmonton Oilers trainer, 1989–2010

I was with the Eskimos, we'd just finished practice, and the Oilers were playing down in Calgary. I was ready to head home, but the game had started. So I sat down and I watched until the end of the first period. We had an offensive side of the room and a defensive side at Commonwealth Stadium. I was on the defensive side, nobody left except offensive guys.

Kevin Lowe got hit. Mr. Mark Hunter caught him with his head down. Kevin had the puck in his feet and he'd just got it away when *wham!* Today it's a major penalty, but not back then.

He was out cold. His one knee just buckled as he went down. And I remember hearing those offensive players in the Eskimos room saying, "Oh, my god. Did you see that hit? He's done."

Well, Bearcat was out there on the ice just as quick as Oilers trainer Peter Millar. I'll never forget that.

I always think of Bearcat as the guy with the big moustache and the big heart. I never worked with Bearcat in the same room, but we worked in the same industry. We were such a fraternity. We worked so closely with each other, in every aspect. I noticed that coming over from football. We were trainers but we were friends, we didn't need to worry about forgetting something because you had a partner on the other end who'd help you out.

Once we got to playoffs, it was kind of different. We shut things down. But just a great group to work with.

What I remember vividly is my first playoffs, going out to have lunch with the Colorado trainers between morning skates, and I'm going, "But we're playing these guys…"

Bearcat was a big part of that. He believed in keeping everyone as safe and healthy as possible. I never heard a bad word about Bearcat.

SHANGRI-LA

I CALL IT SHANGRI-LA because that's exactly what it was. A paradise.

A piece of land owned by George and Betty Rockafellow, about five to eight miles from town. Right on the Bow River. Down from their farm. They'd inherited it.

The best place in the world—and I'm not exaggerating—to fish for rainbow trout. You'd catch 'em and they'd weigh anywhere from two to five pounds. Wonderful to eat, but most of the time we'd release them back into the water.

We'd fly fish most of the time, on the bank or wading into the water, but I had a small boat, too, and we'd go down the river for miles. Just... heaven. Or at least as close to it as you'll get on this earth.

After we moved back here to stay, Shirley and I, and the boys too, spent every summer, all summer, for years and years down there, camping in tents or in our trailer.

We were welcome as could be. We'd wander down on the 24th of May, after the season was done, on the long weekend, and wouldn't come home until we'd be starting to gear up for training camp.

George and Betty are tremendous hockey fans. Their boys were into sports, too, one of them a hockey goalie and another one a high-school football player. And they were all so, so welcoming to us. Every team I ever worked for, the players, coaches, management, you name it, would

head down and spend a day or two, or more, in Shangri-La. They were welcome whenever they wanted to pay a visit.

A lot of the guys I'd bring out would be awestruck. Smokey McLeod was really a nut about the fishing, for instance. Joe Crozier and his wife absolutely loved the place. I remember Rick Wamsley, our goalie, making the trip and those rainbow trout, brother, they'd fight like a mad bull. They'd literally fly out of the water. Well, with Wammer this one time, we were in the boat and I caught a big one. But it wasn't giving up without a fight. I had a drag on the boat and it'd barely move. This trout must've been close to five pounds and I had it on the line a long, long time. It ran and ran and ran, like you see with marlin and swordfish on the ocean.

This turned into a helluva scrap. I finally got the fish in and we'd always rest 'em, then unhook 'em, then let 'em go.

Well, by the time I finally had the son of a gun on the boat, Wammer was there, mouth open wide, and he said, "My god, I've never seen anything like that in my life."

He was absolutely floored.

The fish I did keep, I'd smoke. I had an old smoker but I did the smoking in a cardboard box most of the time. That seemed to hold the flavour better. I'd be smoking these rainbow trout, look up, and there'd be a line-up of people standing there, waiting for their supper. So we'd always run out of fish.

But that, the fishing, was only part of the magic of the whole place. You're BBQing, visiting, camp-firing, playing horseshoes, shooting clay pigeons. People could just show up, relax, and be themselves.

The whole camping and fishing thing was so relaxing for me. It definitely could be considered a de-stressor. We often brought a lot of things other than water to drink, which sure helped with the relaxation.

George and Betty actually weren't big on fly fishing when we first started to go there. But my gang taught 'em and they fell in love with

it, too. I'd scold 'em. "You've got this amazing place within one mile of your home and you let all us people use it!"

But we got 'em thinking our way after awhile.

After we'd won, of course we took the Cup down to Shangri-La—this is before it was structured as it is now—and we enjoyed a helluva party.

As good, if not better, than any of the deals we set up with the Flames.

A BEARCAT Q&A

ED. NOTE: *Questions by coauthor George Johnson and answers by Bearcat Murray.*

Q: Favourite road city?

A: Boston. You betcha. No. 1 with me. Always has been, always will be. You could be stranded out there somewhere to-hell-and-gone like we were at our hotel when we played there, far from downtown, and still walk anywhere. A bald-headed little potlicker like me never had to worry about being hijacked. I felt right at ease all the time there, can't recall one time I didn't, and downtown Boston is *so* interesting. I enjoy history, the architecture.

Another plus, of course, is that the seafood is outstanding.

Q: Best road rink to work in?

A: I'm going to have to say Detroit. The old Joe Louis Arena. We had lots of room there, lots of heat, lots of fans in the room, and I had a big office as trainer. Awesome place to work in. Kind of a junky setup everywhere else by that time, but I loved it. Didn't hurt either that the Little Caesar's guy who owned the place and the Red Wings, Mike Ilitch, had a spot two steps outside our room where it was all-you-could-eat pizza! Can't beat that.

Q: Worst road rink to work in?

A: Boston. The Garden. Just terrible. You'd walk in and there were eight cases of Coca-Cola spilled on the floor and never mopped up so you'd stick to the floor like an old turkey. An old rink that felt like it. Didn't like Toronto's Maple Leaf Gardens a lot, either, but it was better than Boston.

Q: The job of trainer is a multi-tasker. You're a conduit to the coach, looking after the health of the players, listening to their complaints, etc.

A: Well, they've got to trust you. That was most important to me. I'm there for them. I remember once, we had some new guy come in, and I had to explain to him how we did everything. So we sat and talked and he had something going on that was kind of private to him and I told him—I didn't know the guy at all that point—"That's pretty personal stuff. Do you trust me? Let me assure you, I keep my mouth shut. I don't tell any tales out of school."

And he said, "Oh, I know that already, because Al MacInnis has filled me in—that anytime there's anything I need, anything at all, I just go to Bearcat." When I heard that, coming from MacInnis, it made me feel pretty good. Because if Al MacInnis trusts me, I figured, then most of them must trust me.

Q: The highest pain threshold of any player you worked with?

A: Right off the bat, I'm going to say Nick Fotiu. A lot of 'em were good, but he was amazing. New Yorker. Strong as a bull.

Q: Toughest player?

A: Again, Nick Fotiu. Timmy Hunter is right up there, of course. Nobody's doubting his toughness.

I'm talking off-ice stuff here, too—mental toughness, dealing with pain, dealing with sickness, dealing with the wife giving you s—t—and being able to put it aside. Nick just pushed through everything. I'm

pretty sure he was a Golden Gloves boxing champion in New York. I remember him fighting Rick Jodzio while Nick was playing for New England. The WHA days. That was a heckuva scrap. Nick didn't lose many but he lost that one. He always said Jodzio cheated. Jodzio was already in the penalty box and Nick went over to the box to get him, to keep it going. So Jodz was standing on wood, Nick was on ice, and Jodz nailed him, because he had better footing. Jodz was also higher, punching downward.

That's what Nicky was mad about, the advantages Jodz had in that fight.

Tough, Nick. Just bone-tough.

There was a guy played for Medicine Hat, in the senior league. Larry Plante was his name. Nobody else would remember him. But I can't forget him. You remember those 10-cent beer glasses? He'd eat them. I'm serious. Stick 'em in his mouth and chew 'em right up. Unbelievable SOB. I think he was an ex-cop. Big, big man, same as Nick Fotiu.

Q: The most talented player you ever worked with?

A: Oh, Kent Nilsson. Even in practice, you couldn't take your eyes off him. You'd be like, "How the hell did he do *that*?!" I probably could've scored 30 goals at my age back then, playing on his line. It broke my heart the way it ended with him and the Flames. They let him down. Didn't handle him right. It was all over Badger Bob; he wasn't Badger's type of player. Badger'd put him on the fourth line sometimes.

Imagine, a guy that good on the fourth line!

But let's not get into that.

Q: Hardest single loss?

A: The year in juniors with the Centennials when we had all those best-of-nine series, so the owners could make more money, our first series was against Medicine Hat. We had nine bench-clearing brawls in nine games, and we won. Then we played another nine-game series, against

New Westminster, and it went nine games, too, and, oh, we had fights every game. Then we went into the final against Regina. Every game was decided by one goal but they wound up beating us in four straight.

We just had nothing left by then. The tank was completely empty. That broke my heart because the guys played so hard and so well, we'd been through hell through the first 18 games, and we were flat-a—worn out.

Making it worse, the Memorial Cup was in Calgary that year. Today, we'd have qualified automatically—free ride—as host, but not back then.

Q: Favourite opposing player?
A: Oh, boy. There were so damn many of them. Off the top of my head, I'm thinking Bucky, Kelly Buchberger, from Edmonton. Really liked him.

Actually, I liked Gretzky, all those guys.

Q: The most annoying opposing player?
A: Also up in Edmonton. The squeaky little bastard, Ken Linseman. He just drove me up the wall. Drove a lot of people up the wall.

Q: The most underrated player you worked with?
A: Sergei Makarov. He comes to mind. What a talent. He came to us when he was older, of course, and already famous, but this was someone who was good at everything. So skilled. I honestly don't think people here appreciated him the way they should have.

Another guy I thought was a tremendous player who didn't get enough credit was Paul Reinhart.

Q: If you were going to start a team with any one player you were associated with over the years, any level, who would it be?
A: Danny Gare. I love the guy.

Q: Okay, then, on a more general level, who do you choose to spearhead a team—Gordie Howe or Wayne Gretzky?

A: Boy. Automatically, I say Howe. My kind of guy. Tougher'n old shoe leather, didn't take any crap. Guys loved playing with him. Even a little guy like me coulda gone out there and done my thing and not worried about anybody taking any liberties. He'd have looked after me. No one would've touched a hair on my head—if I'd had any.

Q: As someone who treated players for a living and had their best interests at heart, where do you stand on making injuries public? Back in the day, the team would say, "So and so has suffered a fractured ankle and will be out four to six weeks." Now, injuries are more hush-hush than a dossier of CIA secrets.

A: I'm for disclosure. They're hurt. So what? Players get hurt. It's no sin. Let the people know what's going on. I was always against holding back on anything of that nature and the doctors agreed. Some of these guys with the teams didn't want people to even know the players shaved because, well, what would happen if they get a cut?! It was unreal.

Somebody always finds out—might be the stick boy or the guy who digs the holes to put the nets on. Then that somebody is going to let it out, tell somebody else, and then chances are it'll get all screwed up, everybody speculating about how serious the injury is, all that.

Telling people the truth is not going to affect how long it'll take a player to return from an injury. Never has. Never will. But for some reason everybody wants to head off into a corner and start whispering like somebody's just robbed a bank. And it could be an ingrown toenail!

Honesty. They do say it's the best policy.

It's tough when guys get hurt. They're like your kids. You want the best for them. You're talking about health and careers. Injuries scared the hell out of me. That's why I was so observant.

I remember when Jamie Hislop lost sight in an eye at the Corral. Terrible. Sticks can be nasty things and he got clipped. Nothing wild,

more of an accident. A shame. He wasn't the type of guy who'd get involved in crazy stuff. Too smart. And such a good person.

Q: Favourite restaurant on the road?

A: Again, Boston. Right across from our hotel—Legal Sea Foods.

Q: Most memorable fight?

A: I'd have to say the one in the WHA—well, not one, there were so many in the WHA—but that night in Quebec City everyone still talks about, where everyone was brawling and I got 14 stitches under my eye after being kicked in the head by a fan. That was a hummer.

Q: Best atmosphere in a road arena?

A: Any of the Original Six buildings. I enjoyed Toronto. I didn't enjoy the rink and didn't like the team much, but the atmosphere was good, exciting. Saturdays, *Hockey Night in Canada*, all that. Montreal. Chicago. Boston—even though, as I said, it was awful to work in. Any of those places.

Among the newer rinks at the time, Philadelphia was great. Absolutely crazy, those people. Any given night, you didn't know what the hell might happen at the Spectrum.

Q: Who's your favourite player today?

A: Not many, being honest. I guess I'd say our guy, No. 13, Johnny Gaudreau. But I am partial to little guys. We talked once and I asked him, "Does it bother you that people say you're too small to be playing here?" And he said, "Yeah, a little." And I told him what I told Marty St. Louis when he left here, the thing my dad had told me when I was a little guy playing senior men's hockey at 14, 15, 16 years old—"When people talk to you like that, just ask 'em if they'd ever been in bed with a mosquito."

When Tampa Bay beat us in '04, Marty St. Louis found me and told me, "Bear, what you told me, when I was here, I took that to heart. Thought a lot about it. Thanks." Really nice of him to say.

Q: Can you choose one prank among the hundreds, maybe thousands, that you played that remains memorable?

A: Well, I used to have two whirlpools in my area in the back, one hot, one cold, for physiotherapy. Well, one time I switched 'em up the night before. Put the cold water in the hot tub and vice-versa. Lanny and Riser were always in early and had this routine—they'd each go get a coffee, the paper, then head for the tubs.

Well they come rushing in the room with their coffee and their paper, making a rush for the tub. I kind of moved over and got in the way of Lanny, blocked him.

Riser—he had no time to feel the water—figured he had a free pass to the hot tub but mistakenly jumped into the ice-cold whirlpool, 'cause I'd switched them. He went in over his head, underneath, and all of a sudden he comes firing up out of that thing—and I'm taking pictures, I've got my camera ready—water snortin' and blowin' everywhere, and shouts, "Holy s—t! *Tab-er-nac!*"

Well, Lanny spilled his coffee. I just about died laughing. A bit of payback, actually, because those guys were, as I said, throwing me in the big whirlpool all the time. Seemed to me I spent half my time down at the rink soaking wet.

Q: What's the best piece of advice you've ever received?

A: My dad had one saying that's always stuck with me: "Quit standing around. You stand around doin' nothing and some big dog'll come up and p—s all over you." He was right. Don't stand still. Keep moving or something bad might happen.

Q: You are, as everyone is aware, an avid golfer. A favourite course?

A: Banff Springs. When I was 14, 15, 16, we'd go up there and play all day for $10. No such thing as gas carts. Pull cart or carry. What a beautiful golf course. For us back then, that place was king of the hill. I've played on a lot of great courses all over the place since then but to me, to this day, Banff is the greatest.

Q: Pick a dream foursome of pals to play a round with.

A: Right off the bat, my partner at so many charity tournaments—especially the Sutter boys' tournaments over the years—big Doug Barkley. We've been doing them together for 50, 60 years. We've put in lot of miles travelling together when the oil patch was the major contributor to charity, front and centre for the support and money. So Barks, for sure.

I'm afraid I'm going to have to turn this into a fivesome, though, if you're including me.

When I first started golfing, I had four buddies and we'd go to High River and meet the gang from Blackie. The Blackie guys and the Okotoks guys would meet and play all day. Then we switched to Turner Valley. And we did that our whole lives. Every Tuesday.

So I'd have include Jimmy Wilson, my old winger, my friend, my fishing buddy. Bobby McLean, who became my brother-in-law, married my sister. Bobby Jackson. And Cliff Nesselbach.

Bobby's gone. Jimmy's gone. It's tough losing friends you've had your whole life. And all those guys were oil patch people during their working lives. That's how I fell in love with golf. Being with them.

And at the start, the only clubs we could get we had to borrow. I borrowed clubs from a guy I worked with in the grocery store—I delivered groceries—and he had the old-time wooden shafted clubs. But they were left-handed. So the first four years I played, I golfed left-handed.

I can still hit left-handed.

But those were *good* friends. My whole life. So they've gotta be part of any golf group I'm involved in.

Q: You've always been in tip-top physical condition. We who travelled with the team in those years vividly remember you rollerblading around the concourses of various arenas to improve your conditioning and how light you were on your feet when someone injured required attention.

A: Well, I had to practice what I preached to my players, didn't I? I've been that way my whole life, being in shape. When I played, I wasn't a big guy so I had to get every edge I could. And, of course, I worked very hard at it while I was a jockey.

My dad was always after me to work out, to not shy away from the kind of stuff that pushed you. So I was just brought up that way.

I remember going to work on the drilling rigs. I used to climb the derrick every day, shimmy up what they call the fast-line, which is the line that pulls the pipe out of the hole. I'd zip up there like it was a rope, 125 to 130 feet in the air, like it was nuthin'.

The driller would tell me, "We always run into somebody that's crazy."

So it just seemed I've always been active, doing different things that kept me in shape. A way of life, I guess you'd say.

Q: What are your memories of the snowstorm game where only 334 fans showed up in Jersey?

A: That was a tough trip. The damn snowstorm…the bus driver got lost going to the rink, of all things, and he kept going 'round and 'round the building but couldn't find a way in.

That shoulda tipped us off to the way the night was gonna go.

Then the game kept being delayed. But the worst part for Bobby and me was the next day, in the morning at the airport. They threw all our equipment on the sidewalk in front of the depot, it's snowing, the stuff's wet, and we'd traded a guy the night before but they didn't tell us! The game ended so late the equipment never did dry. We did our best but it was still wet. Luckily, Bobby was a master at packing stuff up. He was always great. Never complained. Head down, just went to work.

So we were out on the sidewalk in front of the airport terminal rummaging through the stick bags and equipment bags to find stuff for the guy who had been traded. Everything was laying in the snow, getting even wetter. I was madder'n a SOB. *How dumb are you guys?! You coulda told us last night! Why keep it a secret? You think we're going to go out and tell everybody? I hope we miss this flight because of you guys.*

To this day, for the life of me I can't understand the thinking behind them keeping us in the dark about that.

Q: A favourite among opposition coaches?

A: Well, one guy I really liked was Harry Neale. We were in there, Vancouver, one night when the Canucks weren't doing very well, and he was in deep s—t with the fans. So this one guy's sitting *way* up in the corner somewhere, and he's yelling, "Fire Harry Neale! Fire Harry Neale! Fire Harry Neale!" Over and over and over. Well finally, I'd had enough, stood up on the bench, and started hollering back, "Go home, you a—hole!"

I must've yelled when the building was pretty quiet because Harry heard me. He came over after the game and thanked me.

One of the great coaches in my whole life in hockey lived right in Okotoks, Elmer Piper. Intermediate-senior level. He'd do a lot of his coaching with me in the car between Okotoks and Nanton or Okotoks and somewhere else. He was probably my first real coach outside of my dad.

Q: Over the years, you've met your share of non-hockey celebrities. Anyone pop immediately to mind as standing out from that crowd?

A: I'd say Bobby Curtola, the singer. He'd had a bunch of hit records and someone invited me to a concert of his on a charity thing one time. Well, Bobby was so friendly when we met him that we just took to each other. We became wonderful friends. He even rewrote lyrics to two songs for me, put all the guys' names in there, even mine. One

was for the Calgary Cowboys song that we'd play on the loudspeaker as the team came out on the ice before a game. And then again, same type of thing, for the WHL Wranglers a couple years later. I still have tapes of those songs.

We did a lot of charity events together over the years, Bobby and I. Well, Shirley and her friends just peed themselves, of course, getting the chance to meet Bobby Curtola.

One time Bobby tells me I've got to go Vegas, so I did, with a couple of friends, and he let us use his condo. We stayed there about a week and in the garage he had an old Cadillac. Beautiful car. So I ended up getting pretty p—ed and we decided to go for a drive down the Strip. I felt like Elvis Presley in this car! And I'll be a dirty name if I didn't wind up driving on the wrong side of the road. Finally found a place to make a U-turn and I somehow got that big boat turned around.

Bobby was just a great person. Every friend I had, he went out of his way to make them his friend too.

That's the type of guy he was.

Q: Any other memorable celebrity run-ins?

A: Well, the one night in Chicago, we're backing the bus out of the old Stadium after a game but this car is blocking our way. And someone says, "That's John Candy's limo." Big, long thing. And, you know me, I'm grumbling, "We've got to get out of here. Who does that f—ing potlicker think he is?!" So I hop off the bus, march up the ramp to the limo, and knock on the window. Candy rolls down the window, recognizes me, and invites me into the car to talk.

The guys on the bus, I'm sure, were madder'n hell, sitting there.

We had a great conversation. Helluva nice guy.

I met Rocky, Sylvester Stallone, in L.A.—just a little tiny guy, way smaller than you'd imagine—and we became friends.

Hoyt Axton, the country singer, was just a wonderful person. Heavyset fella, ended up dying in 1999 of a heart attack. I'd always arrange for

tickets for him when we played in L.A. I wondered, *Okay, where do you sit him?* So I started by getting him tickets behind the bench. Turned out he didn't like that because everybody recognized him from the movies and his TV appearances and started bugging him for autographs and stuff. So we found somewhere else for him to sit.

Turned out, his mother was more famous than he was. Mae Boen Axton co-wrote, among other chart-toppers, "Heartbreak Hotel" for Elvis Presley! And for some reason he'd always be trying to get me into the movies. He'd say, "We'll just fly you down and fly you back." Ended up he bought a church camp out in Montana near where they shot *A River Runs Through It* and turned it into a movie/TV studio. He kept saying, "You're gonna have to change your job. I want you down here." Guess he wanted me to play the sidekick to the hero or something. He'd always say, "Well, ya little potlicker, you can't sing or dance but we'll find something for you to do!"

Then it all fell through because he had the heart attack and died. God, that Hoyt, what a good guy.

Another person I became good friends with was Jamie Farr, from the TV series *M*A*S*H*. A big hockey fan. He was here doing a show, at the Stage West dinner theatre I believe, and we were invited to go. We met him after the show in his dressing room. We had golf in common. He really helped Dinah Shore, the singer, at her tournament in California, and ended up running it. So golf was our connection. We hit it off, corresponded often, and every time he came to town he would call. I knew the TV show and really enjoyed it, the way everyone did back then. One time we went out to the golf course, I think my son Danny went with us to play.

Jamie and I, we kept in touch for a long time.

Q: The worst flier/flight in your experience?

A: I'd have to say the worst flier was Donny Tannahill, in World Hockey. We had a terrible, terrible flight this one trip. We were on a DC-6,

just a rattletrap. We might've been coming home from New England for a game the next night. Anyway, I couldn't see out the window! I always got a window seat. But I couldn't see a thing. *What the hell's going on?* Donny Tannahill was just going nuts. It was black on the window. Just black. Oil. We weren't leaking gas; we were leaking oil. I was talking to Joe Crozier, the coach, and we headed up to talk to the pilot. Well, it's as if they had picked somebody at random off the street to fly the plane. Anyway, we stopped in London, Ontario, to fill up with oil. They were up on the wing pouring it into the motor. I mean, this was crazy.

We'd land periodically to get new oil. Finally, we landed in Fargo, North Dakota. Joe sent me into the terminal to see if there were any other planes available. The girl in there told me there was one coming in at 7:00 AM—it was 4:00 AM then—and she told me we could fly to Denver with that plane, then change and get back to Calgary.

So she booked us on this flight and the guys were hugging me, kissing me on the cheek. We had to wait the three hours, so the guys were sleeping on the floor in the terminal, waiting for this plane to arrive. I had to get the equipment off the one plane and then onto the other. Just a mess.

We were luckier than hell we didn't crash at some point, with that oil leaking onto the windows. That was the worst, the scariest. In my experience, anyway.

Q: You've got a couple of the best nicknames in the game, "Bearcat" and "Potlicker." What's another that you're especially fond of?

A: The Magic Man, for Kent Nilsson. Said it all about him.

Q: Players like things just so. Athletes are notorious for idiosyncrasies and rituals. Care to share any?

A: So many guys had something going on in that regard. But here's one: every game, home and away, Timmy Hunter had nine sticks on the rack. *Nine.* You'd think maybe a goal-scorer or a playmaker,

171

a Nieuwendyk or a Gilmour, right? Nope. Timmy Hunter. He'd go through those nine sticks 10 times during a game. He was unbelievable. Used to tick me off because his sticks took up the whole rack. And then he'd be fiddling with them the whole game. When you'd go on the road, you'd need one bag just for his sticks.

Tim also had this ritual: he'd come in for practice every morning, get into his underwear, and come into the training room. I had this big tray in the room with nail clippers, files, scissors, a wax machine—almost like a beauty parlour. Well, every day he'd come in and meticulously cut his nails with the clippers. Clip, clip, clip. Then he'd do it again before a game. Clip, clip, clip.

Why? Because he didn't want to cut anybody. He knew more likely than not he'd have to drop his gloves and fight during the game that night and if he cut someone he was out, ejected automatically. So he was very particular about his nails being short. That was part of his preparation.

Sarge, Brad McCrimmon, had to have his stuff hanging. He'd watch to make sure it was there, hanging in his dressing stall. The team would be leaving for a game somewhere else the next night and we, the guys under orders to get the gear together to get out quick, had to wait until Brad left the room until we stuffed it in a bag because he didn't want it packed. Well, we had to pack it, right? I loved the man, we all did, but he had his little peculiarities when it came to equipment and things.

Another guy that comes to mind is Doug Gilmour. He didn't like Steri-Strips, those things like little Band-Aids that you'd put on cuts. Now you can't let a guy who's been cut on the ice without one. But Killer, he'd rather have just bled all over everything. You could get away with those a lot of times rather than stitches and in some cases they would actually do a better job. I'd tell him, "You can't go out there bleeding!" and he'd get really p—ed off. Just leave him alone; didn't want you fooling with him.

Q: Best friend(s) you made in hockey?

A: Oh, too many to count. Right off the bat…Phil Russell, Rusty Patenaude, Smokey McLeod, a bunch of those guys from the Cowboys, like Donny Tannahill. Danny Gare, of course. Lanny, that whole gang from '89. John Davidson. Back in the early days, Cec Papke, who started me out as a trainer. I played hockey with him; he played centre for me in the senior league. And we worked in the oil patch together. Wonderful, wonderful friend, Cec. That included work and play.

Q: Favourite expression?

A: "I wouldn't give him a seat on the bus." I'd use it for any player that I wasn't too keen on, for whatever reason. Goes back to my days driving the bus in junior. That became my favourite expression.

I remember sitting in a game at the Saddledome not that long ago, in the stands, and the guy next to me mentioned this certain player. I won't mention any names. And I told him, "I wouldn't give him a seat on the bus." I explained what I meant and the guy said, "Why?" Well, I don't like talking against guys—I'd never worked with this one, I really didn't know him at all—but as a trainer I had to isolate people on the ice. I'd read the play, in the corners, and recognize players who put themselves at risk or make a mistake. Because my whole career was watching individual instances. So I told this guy beside me, "Okay, you watch so-and-so. Just him. Don't take your eyes off him. You do, and you'll miss all the mistakes he makes." So one time the guy quit skating; another time he lost the puck in a bad spot; another time he had a bad change. And sure enough, after a while, the guy sitting next to me said, "Holy s—t. You're right!"

And I told him, "See. *That's* why I wouldn't give him a seat on the bus!"

Q: Knowing you're a big fan of Western movies, name a favourite duster?

A: *Broken Arrow* with Jimmy Stewart. I loved the guy who was the chief, Jeff Chandler, in that. He was good in all his movies. And the

173

Apache girl played by Debra Paget Jimmy Stewart married was just a gorgeous, gorgeous lady.

Q: Best aspect of being a trainer?

A: Helping players. Having the knowledge and the ability to assist them through various injuries.

There's no worse feeling than not being able to play. I knew that from the days I played. So for me to be able to help them through those difficult times, get them back on the ice as soon as possible…it was an amazing thing.

Q: The worst part of being a trainer?

A: The worry of not being able to do my job. I was scared all the time. Health for those guys is such an important thing. To them and to the success of the team. I studied and studied, talked to people, got people to help me be better at my job, paramedics, doctors. I bugged the hell out of them and had literally hundreds of teachers who were all so willing to help.

So the worry of maybe not being able to help, I'd say that would be it.

I've had to deal with a number of serious situations. I've talked about a few of them. But one time, when I was with the Centennials, a guy named Rob Tudor from the Regina Pats went down and slid right into Bobby Nystrom. He took Bobby's feet right out from underneath him. Well, this guy just laid there on the ice and then started to go into convulsions. Their trainer was an old guy and he was down by where the Zamboni comes in. He couldn't get the door open.

So I just said to hell with it and jumped out on the ice.

We carry forceps and an oral screw, a plastic gizmo that helps open the mouth and keep it open. Anyway, Rob Tudor had swallowed his tongue. So I helped him out. Matter of fact, when Shirley and I celebrated our 60th anniversary awhile back, had a bit of a party, this guy stood up and

told the story, thanked me for saving his life. Well, I didn't save his life. What I did was my job. But it was nice of him to acknowledge it.

The very same thing happened to Eddy Beers, our big winger with the Flames. He went down in the corner in Buffalo one time, got jammed into the boards, and went into convulsions. As soon as he went down, I was out there. You can tell when something's serious. I got over to him and I remember Eddy gasped out, "Hurry. Hurry." Well, that's what you've been trained for, so your knowledge and instincts take over.

Those sorts of incidents are scary, though. But that's the job, dealing with situations of that nature. It's what you signed up for.

Q: You're someone who's spent a good deal of his life helping people in physical distress. What's the scariest injury you sustained during your training career?

A: During a game in Minnesota, at the old Met Centre. I was on the bench in front of the North Stars' blueline, game was on. I was behind the players, bringing water, and I peeked up to see Gary Roberts shoot the puck into their end. *Okay, good, puck's gone.*

Then, *boom!* All of a sudden I was on my a—.

This little defenceman of theirs had stopped the puck, shot it out right away, but Gary was still standing right there and damn if he didn't deflect the puck up and it hit me right underneath the left eye, lower cheek.

Twenty-one stitches it took to close. Blood *everywhere.* At first, I thought I'd lost the eye. It was scary. I ended up on the floor, got hauled into the room, and the next thing I knew the ex-trainer of Minnesota, who was retired but had been in the stands watching the game, was there to help the doc. I couldn't have been in better hands.

We had a charter plane that night, going to Toronto, I believe. I sure wasn't staying in Minny, but after the plane took off I couldn't stop throwing up, because of all the blood I'd swallowed from the cut. I was miserable as hell.

After I got looked at in Toronto, I just caught the next flight home. Everybody then checked me out after I got to Calgary. Our doctors here thought they'd have to do some surgery. My cousin, a plastic surgeon, had a look at me.

The whole thing wound up turning out okay but it was no fun. Weird thing was it was the opposite eye of the one the guy who kicked me in the face during that WHA brawl in Quebec City had hit.

So I guess I've got a matching set.

Q: Understanding this is going to be a hellish assignment, but try and select a personal All-Star team, Flames only, from your 16 years working at first the Corral and then the Saddledome. Let's start at centre ice.

A: I'd say Doug Gilmour, Joe Nieuwendyk, and Kent Nilsson. I really enjoyed watching them. Skating, stickhandling, scoring goals. My type of players. I got along great with Robert Reichel, too. But those three I mentioned before just stand out. Excellent, the three of them.

Q: Right wing is a particularly difficult ask. There's a slew of top-drawer options at that position. The usual suspects, of course, but also the formidable talents the quality of, say, Sergei Makarov, an NHL Hall of Famer.

A: Well, Lanny, for sure. Joe Mullen and Hakan Loob, too. Gotta have those guys. They meant so much to us winning in '89. But that leaves out Theo and I love Theo. So it's tough. Holy mackerel. I'm putting four on my team.

Q: On left wing?

A: Well, right off the bat, Gary Roberts. As I told you, I think Colin Patterson was a really, really underrated guy. So he's there. I like Bobby MacMillan but I really liked the Big Train, Eric Vail, too. So those four.

Q: Okay, we'll concede you that. Need at least four defencemen, preferably six.

A: Al MacInnis, for sure. Phil Russell, for sure. Gary Suter. Beast—Brad McCrimmon. Paul Reinhart, very talented guy. And even though he wasn't with us long, I'm going to say Rob Ramage.

Q: In goal, who gets the nod as backup to Mike Vernon?

A: Well, Mikey's automatic, of course. I thought Reggie Lemelin, Don Edwards, and Wammer—Rick Wamsley—were all really good. Can't choose between 'em. Mikey's gonna play most of the time anyway, right?

SNAPSHOTS

GORDIE HOWE

Back in 1974, the WHA had put together an All-Star team that was preparing for a series against the Russians. And they were playing games against a Western Hockey League All-Star team to get ready for that.

I was the trainer for the juniors, all by myself. Did everything. Sharpened skates, hauled equipment. Whatever needed doing. Anyway, we played a game somewhere and had to catch a plane to the city where the next game was being held. Of course it happened to be pouring rain.

Well, the guy with the truck carrying our equipment and I, out on the tarmac, had to wait until they loaded the pro stuff onto the plane. So we waited and we waited.

All of sudden, it was our turn.

Well, while we were doing this, everybody working there took off. Gone. The airplane people, everybody. So me and the truck driver were loading our equipment on, as fast as we could.

Well, the damn plane—I think it was a DC-6—started moving! And I wasn't even on it. So I started waving my arms, got them to stop, rushed onto the plane, and the stewardess said, "Sit down! We're taking off!"

I was soaking wet and running up and down the aisle. Every seat was taken. No seats. The stewardess started to yell at me to sit down. *Okay, where?!*

So Gordie Howe grabbed me and said, 'Sit here!' He put me on his lap and did the seat belt up around both of us. Then we were up in the air! Might've saved my life. Well, Bobby Hull was sitting beside us. And Gordie was telling me, "Hey, old fella, take it easy."

Old fella?! He was older'n me!

Anyway, we were in the air, I was sitting on Gordie's lap, all buckled up and dripping all over the place, and he turned to Bobby and said, "Look at the old fella here. We've got to get him one of your transplants. Needs some hair. And he's soaking wet!" Bobby at this time was selling hair transplants!'

Finally, the pilot called me up and I sat on a little seat right behind him for the rest of the flight—which must've pleased Gordie, because he was absolutely soaked by then.

But from then on, whenever I'd see Gordie, he'd grin and ask, "Got your hair yet?"

Boy, he saved me on that flight, because they weren't waiting, I had nowhere to sit, and they were on the move when Gordie strapped that belt on me.

Wonderful guy, Gordie. He really treated me well. I had a few occasions where we were at charity events together and I felt I was in a position that I could call him my friend. That still makes me feel pretty damned proud.

LANNY MCDONALD

When Cliff Fletcher made the deal on November 25, 1981, to bring Lanny back to Calgary, I was maybe the happiest guy in the world.

We'd lost him once, back in the Centennials days, to Medicine Hat—something that I knew bothered Scotty Munro for a long time afterward.

The class, the leadership, the presence, and that goal-scoring ability…I knew we'd added something very, very special to our team. We lost a couple of good guys, good players—Bobby MacMillan and Tom

Lysiak—in that deal. But I knew from firsthand experience that we were getting a helluva player, and person, in return.

Lanny had enjoyed some great years in Toronto and then Colorado, of course, but coming back home, where he belonged, being an Alberta boy, I had a special feeling about what might happen.

And 1989 proved it.

We've played pranks on each other for as long as I can remember. Even after he'd retired. One time, I remember, he took over that job—vice president in charge of corporate and community affairs—and, hoo boy, he was really ticked off. He wanted to be GM, didn't happen—still don't know why—and he was really hurt.

They put him in this office and he had a rocking horse in there. And, remember, he wasn't a happy camper at the time. Well, I went to visit him in the office one summer day, looked out the window, and the gals who been selected Stampede Queens that year were outside his window, riding their horses around the grass.

Anyway, Lanny left the office for some reason, so I went over and grabbed that damn rocking horse, put it on his desk, took the tail out and turned it upside down so it's sticking in the air, then stuck the tail back on.

Then I went outside where the girls had been riding, picked up a whole bunch of horse s—t that had dropped, put it in one of those cardboard Coke flats, went back up, and dumped it all over on top of his desk, underneath the rocking horse tail sticking in the air.

Then I walked out.

I came in the next day and the girls in the office see me and started laughing. "Bear, you gotta see this! You missed the whole thing!" Well, Lanny had come into the office—not in a good mood anyway, and the stink in there—he hadn't returned to the office after I left the day before and, remember, it's summer, July, and hot—was unbelievable. The whole office stunk!

Anyway, everybody had to get the hell out until they fumigated the place; aired it out.

I was the culprit. And I was in deep s—t, to to speak. But only for a little while.

Lanny has always been a wonderful, wonderful friend to me.

As I mentioned, I still remember when we—the Centennials—lost him to Medicine Hat. Just like with the Vegas Golden Knights in that expansion draft a couple of years ago, you could only protect so many players. Well, we ended up losing Tom Lysiak and Lanny, among others. And it made that Medicine Hat team, turned 'em into a powerhouse. An instant contender.

Lanny thought the reason Scotty didn't protect him is because he'd laughed at Scotty—he was so fat and stuff—one time when Scotty was trying to tie up his skates. Lanny still swears that's what did him in. But it wasn't that. Our head coach in Kamloops (in the BCJHL) at the time, where we got a lot of our players from, said that a guy named John Senkpiel was way better than Lanny. He was convinced of it and kept telling everybody in the organization. So it ended up that we didn't protect Lanny! Gawd, he was upset. We all were.

When he first came here from the farm, from the sticks, he was just a helluva guy. Same as today. Genuine. Down-to-earth. He fit in with the guys right away—a joker, an instigator, and, of course, a helluva player. So everybody liked Lanny right away.

The thing that makes Lanny special—then, now, always—is his attitude. My dad always told me that—you can control your attitude. I'd have a friend and my dad would tell me, "Watch that guy, he's got a bad attitude." And I'd say, "Dad, what are you talking about?" But he always turned out to be right.

Danny Gare was the same way as Lanny. What you noticed first, immediately, was the way they acted, the way they carried themselves.

Lanny makes you feel wanted; makes you feel that he's interested in you. Someone comes up on the street for an autograph or a chat, and he makes them feel like his brother or his sister.

The thing is, people in the public eye are put there by the fans in the first place. And they *want* to like their heroes. Everyone does. When I was a little potlicker, a jockey on the circuit, I'd meet these guys I'd heard about and it was important to me that I liked them. And most of them, I did.

As I said, it all comes down to attitude.

Lanny grabs people by the heart and they just…melt. You have a bad experience with someone you look up to, and that never goes away. Same if you have a good experience. Lanny understands that. You've got to accept people and you've got to appreciate them in order for them to like you.

But he's not out to be liked. It's not an objective. That's just the way he is.

LANNY McDONALD
Calgary Flames, 1981–89

When I first joined the Calgary Centennials, Bearcat took me under his wing. Probably because he saw how raw I was. Actually, raw might be a gross understatement. Right off the farm. No clue.

So Bearcat, bless him, showed me the ropes and made me feel comfortable, from the first day I met him. Years later, when I got traded to the Flames, he was the trainer, of course, and he just assumed I'd be going back to the No. 7 from my Toronto days. Well, I'd worn No. 9 in Colorado— Gordie Howe's number; of course, he was one of my favourites—so I'd taken quite a shine to it.

The Flames had traded away Randy Holt, the tough guy, so No. 7 was available. I got to the rink late in the afternoon—we were playing that night—and Bearcat had the No. 7 jersey all ready for me.

Well, he saw the look on my face and without hesitation said, "We can have that off in no time flat." And he did. I don't know how they got it off

185

the jersey and a new name bar sewn on that quick—I'm sure Bearcat had to sew it on himself by hand—but there I was, wearing No. 9 a couple hours later, making my Flames debut at the Saddledome.

To go full-circle, from the Centennials to the NHL, to Toronto, then to Colorado and back to Calgary and to be able to hook back up again with Bearcat, 10 years later?

Small world.

CEC PAPKE

Cec, as I tell anyone who'll listen, is the reason I'm a trainer.

A very, very good friend of mine. Always telling jokes, playing jokes, talking loud. I first got to know him when we played on a team together in Didsbury, in the Central Alberta League—I only played the home games.

This was at the same time I played here, every game, for the Okotoks Oilers. So I was a busy guy, with all that hockey.

When I began working in the oil business, in Estevan, Saskatchewan, Cec was located in Virden, Manitoba, and while living there, he rented in the same building as my very good friend here in Okotoks, Jimmy Wilson. So when I'd go to Virden—it was part of my territory as a salesman and I had to travel there quite often—I'd visit them both.

Well, wouldn't you know it, Cec ended up in Estevan and we spent eight years together over there. We lived right next door to Cec; his wife, Shirley; and their boys.

Fortunately, in Estevan at that time everybody in the oil patch was doing well. Business was booming.

Cec used to phone me up in the middle of the night. I had a key for his warehouse because I helped him getting bits out to what you might call a "competitor," as I sold one type of bit myself. So he'd call and I'd load up these bits and take 'em out to the rig for him because he was crying in his beer that he couldn't do it, for some unknown reason.

But I knew him, he was a friend, and so I did it. Many, many times, *my* Shirley wanted to know why I'd agree to those trips, those middle-of-the-night phone calls, seeing as how I was, in a way, involved in the same business.

And I told her, "Yeah, but when I'm out delivering Cec's bits to those rigs I'm selling *my* bits too."

I sold a lot of bits on my trips out to those rigs, let me tell you. Little did Cec know.

So Cec and I, we worked together, played together, lived next to each other.

Then I transferred back to Calgary. Cec had been moved back, too, but he quit his job. Then he came to me one day, a very big day for me as things turned out, and said, "Bearcat, I need your help. Two friends and myself have bought the junior Buffaloes hockey team and they're forming a new league called the Western Canada Major Junior Hockey League"—which is now the Western Hockey League—"and I need you to be my trainer."

I was floored. I told him, "Cec, I haven't been a trainer since I was 15, 16 years old and a jockey helping the trainers with the racehorses."

He said, "Doesn't matter. We need you."

So I quit my job—that was in 1967—and went to work for them. That's where my whole career started. Bingo.

People like Cec, Scotty Munro, Alec Recsky…together, they're the reason I took the path in life that I did.

SCOTTY MUNRO

I loved Scotty. But he was really tough on the kids. You wouldn't believe how tough. He explained the way he was by saying, "Bear, I gotta teach 'em. Nobody else will."

To me, he would've been a great father figure for any young person. He had control of things, like a good father would. And he did what

he thought was right—to heck with anybody else. He was tough, but honest, and although it may not have seemed so at the time, he cared.

Whether you were a rookie or a vet, if you ever got any headlines… you were gonna get blasted. Guaranteed. Might as well start ducking. He was a master at that. One time, Danny Gare had been playing really great—at the time he was on that famous line with Mike Rogers and Jerry Holland. Well, Danny had another exceptional night this night, so after the game everybody was busy patting him on the back.

Scotty, true to form, never said a word.

Next morning before practice I was in there getting everything ready to go. Scotty walked in, newspaper rolled under his arm. He strolled right over to Danny and said, "Gare!" Took that newspaper and threw it at him—of course it came apart in the air, like the newspaper boy throwing it on your front step and the pages ending up all over the yard.

Then he said, "This newspaper and these headlines will wrap tomorrow's garbage!" That was a standard saying of his.

I knew it was coming. I almost wanted to run and hide. Because the kid—whoever he might be—was up, feeling good about himself. He'd had a good night. And then, *wham!*, he gets knocked to his knees in front of everybody in the middle of the room.

Didn't matter what your name was.

But then, sure as shooting, Scotty would go back, on the quiet, put his arm around the kid, and console him.

He had the kid's heart in mind, but he acted the way he did because he knew if you started letting them get away with that crap—believing those headlines, for instance—pretty soon they're a cocky little SOB. "Can't have that in the dressing room, Bear," he'd say.

That's the way he was.

These kids are not at home, remember; they're older teenagers and someone's got to be responsible for them, teach them the right way to do things. And Scotty made bloody sure they'd learned before they left. Many of the guys who wound up turning pro will tell you that.

Another time, I remember, we were in Medicine Hat and we had this one rookie who screwed up on the ice during a game. Screwed up bad. Well, Scotty decided to cut him, then and there.

In the room, he chewed the kid out pretty good. I was almost crying. It hurt just watching. So I just headed out of there. Couldn't take it. But the kid stood there and took it. Of course, I had to get the bus ready, the equipment on, this and that, so I couldn't go console him. Scotty didn't want me doing it anyway. He said, "That's my job, Bear. I'm the guy who had to let him down. So don't interfere."

And sure enough, after we'd driven home and gotten off the bus I saw Scotty put his arm around the kid. They walked into the dressing room together and everything was tickety-boo. He told me, "You'll notice, I'll never, *ever*, let a kid go to bed without talking to him. I'll never, *ever*, let him go to bed feeling sorry for himself."

And it's true. He never did.

A lot of the kids didn't like Scotty's methods, obviously, and talked about them later in life. But they were better off for it.

I came to realize what Scotty meant, and to realize that what he did for the kids was incredible. Eventually, I got the point. It took me awhile to quit crying, but eventually, I understood.

He brought kids up out of the boondocks and helped turn them into men.

ALEC RECSKY

Alec's the reason I became a trainer. I cannot say enough about him personally, about what he meant to me, to my career, to my life.

Hanging around Alec...I could not have received a better education in my field if I'd gone to college for 20 years. He was generous with his time and with his knowledge. Alec grew up here, worked for the YMCA, then at a private place. That didn't pan out. Too many people telling him what and what not to do.

189

I met him after I'd started with the Centennials, through the training pipeline. And we just hit it off, as you do with some people. The two of us, along with a guy named Larry Chase, would visit high schools and talk to the kids about injuries, prevention, nutrition, and such. Then he got me hooked up with the Stampeders, which turned out to be an education in itself.

Alec knew everybody in the field. We'd visit hospitals to study the doctors. Sometimes we were allowed into the OR to watch them work on knees and such.

Alec said to me once, "Bear, don't let anybody kid you. You've got 40 professors working with you, not three!"

We're friends. I'm proud to be able to say that. He just turned 90 in 2020. What a man!

He ended up buying a beautiful place in Kelowna. Shirley and I would go and visit him. He worked at lot with the university out there, even after retiring. I bought a motor home here in Okotoks, from a school teacher. I'd drive out to Southern B.C., the Kelowna area, and we'd play 36 holes of golf a day. Every day, a different course.

We were always joking. The damn motor home has a narrow top on it; can't sit up in bed or nothing. Alec's son and two of his friends would pile in with us, and we'd head out to golf for a week. The young guys were down on the side, on a chesterfield and the floor, to sleep. Alec and I were in the top bin, I call it. So he crawled in there this one night, and I winked at the other guys.

"Okay, it's my turn."

So I stripped down to my shorts, pulled out my false teeth, and I yelled at him, "Okay, honey, I'm coming to get ya!" Well, Alec almost passed out.

There's no way I could ever repay Alec Recsky. Not in a million years. For his friendship. For sharing his knowledge. For his mentoring. I'm so grateful he took me under his wing. Otherwise I never would've made it. I would've had a much different life. I owe him so much.

GARY ROBERTS

Everybody remembers Gary Roberts' first fitness test, in July. It was a kind of run-through, to let the young guys know what to expect at training camp in September. That was one of the good things Badger Bob started, bringing all those guys into town so they could understand what it was gonna take.

Well, Robs had been a first-round pick, remember, so there were a lot of eyes on him. And he failed the tests. Flat-out failed them.

Gary was embarrassed. And Badger's reaction? Devastated. No other word to use. Crestfallen, maybe.

Wish I had it on tape.

Turned into a helluva player, though, Robs. A little ornery, but in the right way. Big, big heart. Would fight anybody. And look what he's doing now, in retirement. He's one of the most-sought-after high-performance fitness people around, with players flocking to work with him. He's tops in the field, after failing those tests back when he was a kid. Amazing.

The quadricep hematoma he suffered in 1993 was one of the worst injuries I ever encountered. He got kneed by Garry Galley against Philadelphia, and we were playing in Toronto next. Well, Robs was on the plane after the game, moaning and groaning. And this, remember, is a tough kid. Never complained. Nothing. And nobody seemed to be paying any attention! He hadn't even been taped up or anything! With the pressure of being in the plane, up in the air, and that type of injury...I can't imagine the pain.

I'm glad I got off my a— and went to check on him because I love the guy. I took one look and I was thinking, *Holy crap, this is serious*. I'd suffered a couple, maybe three, really bad charley horses during the years that I'd played and you could just tell this was awful. Potentially big trouble.

So I high-tailed it up to the pilot and asked him why were circling for a landing. He told me, "On account of all the air traffic. We might be here all night."

191

So I told him, "I've got a major problem here. There's a player on board hurt. Bad. We *have* to get down." And he said, "That's all I need to know."

I let him know I'd like to have an ambulance meet us on the tarmac. The stewardess got me what I needed—ice packs, towels. I phoned the Toronto doctor and told him to meet us at the hospital. The pilot, great guy, took care of customs.

We actually had three players hurt that night—Brian Skrudland was one of them—who needed attention when we got the plane down.

Well, we landed but there was no ambulance. Not even a limo. Just a damn taxi. We had four guys crowd into it—including me—and off we go to the hospital. The doc was waiting for us as we pulled up to Emergency. What a great guy. He knew it was bad right away. The leg was swollen up, as if Gary had been kicked by a bull.

When we got into a room the doc hit that leg with a knife and, *pow!*, it just exploded. Blood and stuff all over the place. It ended up poor Gary needed surgery to repair a broken blood vessel in his thigh. Under different circumstances, he could've lost that leg. Scares me to even think about now, all these years later.

Typical of Robs, he persevered but then wound up suffering a neck injury from an accumulation of things. Sure, he played hard all the time, and there's a risk in that, but the constant punishment he took from cross-checks was nothing short of incredible. Same thing goes for his pal Joe Nieuwendyk. How could something *not* happen—in Gary's case, nerve damage in the neck—when a guy's taking that amount of pounding night after night?

And nobody did a damn thing about it. I was so mad at the referees. They just stood there and watched.

So he came back, then quit the one time, thought he was done. But he came back again and extended his career quite a few years after that.

As I said, tough kid. Stubborn. I think the world of him.

GARY ROBERTS
Calgary Flames, 1986–96

I remember being in the back of a taxicab, heading to Wellesley Hospital in Toronto after my quadricep injury.

Brian Skrudland was in the front seat and I was laying across Bearcat Murray in the back seat, my leg sticking out the window and about to explode because I'd gotten on that plane with a quadricep hematoma.

If it wasn't for Bearcat that night, helping me, consoling me…I was in so much pain that I was literally screaming at these guys, "Get a knife, I'm cutting this f—ing thing open!" He was with me in the cab and stayed with me all night at the hospital until they cut my quad open to release the pressure.

Also in Toronto, I got hit from behind by Bob Rouse at Maple Leaf Gardens and was taken off on a stretcher. Who's in the ambulance with me, cutting off my equipment as we raced to Wellesley Hospital? Bearcat Murray. I couldn't feel my extremities and he was cutting my equipment off before they put me in the MRI machine for a CAT scan.

Those are both career-ending injuries if you don't have someone there caring for you. And Bearcat was there for me.

I owe Bearcat a huge debt.

I'm such a fitness nut now, of course. Well, Bearcat set an example for me even there, watching him unpack his rollerblades in every arena in the National Hockey League. So you think about his mentality, the energy he brought every day. He was an extremely fit person and he expressed that—not in a preachy way but by doing it every single day.

He helped me with everything—even my putting. I'm such a horses—t putter, and he'd tell me, "Robs, just close your eyes, relax. Breathe in, breathe out. Visualize the ball going in the hole." I was going to the golf course and closing my eyes to putt because Bearcat told me to. That's how much I trusted him. And I'll be honest with you, still, today, there are times when I get the yips putting, I close my eyes and think of Bearcat Murray.

This is back when athletic trainers did it all. They didn't follow a textbook. They just worked. He was far more than an athletic trainer. I don't care how many letters there are behind your name on your business card, there's no second Bearcat Murray as far as the human being he is and how he treated everyone he met.

They don't come any better.

DON (SMOKEY) MCLEOD

A helluva goalie, Smokey. He got his nickname because he came from Trail, British Columbia, and played for the Smoke Eaters.

He was wonderful guy, treated everybody great, such a sweet disposition, but he was a drinker—Canadian Club whiskey, mostly. We had to put C.C. on his helmet. Geez, he even named his German Shepherd C.C. Oh, boy.

One time in Toronto, we came in after dinner and there was Joe Crozier in the hotel with his back against the far wall and his feet on Smokey's door, because he didn't want him sneaking back in. Joe didn't drink, so he was sitting there with a Coke.

It was after curfew, and he was all upset because we were fighting for first place and he was moaning, "Smokey's out. Now I'll have to suspend him and we'll never make it."

Well, I finally came up with a solution. I said, "Joe, he's already going to be fined for being late for curfew. The best thing now is we get up and you leave your Coke can by the door. You don't want to suspend him, but you do want to fine him. Let him know he made a mistake but don't hurt the team. Just walk away."

And Joe said, "Okay. That's a helluva good idea."

Well, turned out Smokey had been visiting his sister! He'd stayed out late but wasn't drinking. When he got back to the hotel he called me in my room. "What's all this crap?" And I told him he was in trouble.

Anyway, we got through it.

An unbelievable goalie. Could handle that puck as well as any goalie I've ever seen. Hell, as good as any defenceman. Had a little hook on his stick. I still have half a dozen of 'em out in my shed. I was convinced he'd score a goal one day.

He was the hero for the Cowboys, right off the bat. People just naturally gravitated to him, liked him. He had that kind of nature.

His wife—they split up, I think she's back in Trail. She was a sweetheart but she wouldn't take any crap from him.

He treated us really, really good. We used to take him down to our river hideaway, Shangri-La, and he'd kind of take over.

When Smokey died in 2015, at 68, it was a sad day. He had his problems, like a lot of people do, but I consider him a great, great friend.

BRAD McCRIMMON

I talked about Nick Fotiu being maybe the toughest guy I ever worked with. By that, I mean physically—dealing with injuries.

But Beast, Brad McCrimmon, he was right up there. On all levels. You see some of the pictures of him from '89, the night we won, and his faced looked like hamburger. Blood dripping. All stitched up. Some of the crap he took—they were always trying to goad him into something—well, I would've gone crazy.

Didn't matter. He took it. And Brad wasn't big on taking crap. But he never retaliated. Such outstanding discipline.

And that discipline rubbed off on the rest of the guys, like, *If Beast can take it, so can I.* That really did it for us.

I remember looking at him one time and saying, "Geez, Beast, you're a *mess!*" And he said, "Leave me alone, Bear, I'm doing fine."

Never complained.

I knew him and his brother Kelly from back in their junior days. Both good, big-hearted, solid, small-town Saskatchewan guys.

The weird thing? He was afraid of flying. Not much scared Beast, but planes did. He was never really comfortable in the air. He might not have shown it, but he'd get very nervous.

Then you look at the way he died, in that plane crash in Russia, coaching KHL Lokomotiv Yaroslavl on September 7, 2011, with 43 others, on takeoff.

That still really bothers me. I hope he didn't know what was going on. Unreal. So, so sad.

ELMER PIPER

I worked with a lot of coaches over the years—more than I can count, or care to remember—but I keep coming back to Elmer Piper.

To me, he's probably the man who's most knowledgeable about the hockey business.

Pipe owned an Esso service station—they did some repairs there but mostly just sold gas—and I swear to god that the Russians, who would've seen Ernie's team during the Trail Smoke Eaters days, copied his methods, the methods they were using when they were kicking our a—.

Poor old Pipe had Coke bottle glasses and he'd be driving this great big Cadillac. Not quite sure how he managed it.

Anyway, what a hockey mind. He was a Scotty Bowman around here. A stalwart. He had a way, Elmer, of giving this amazing advice to players. Me, for instance.

When I played for Pipe, there was one guy—played for Claresholm—I just couldn't figure out. Stopped me every time. Spitting image of Jean Beliveau, this guy. Seemed eight feet tall to me. A defenceman. I could skate like the wind—a bit cocky, I suppose—but I had a helluva time against this guy whenever we'd be up against each other on the ice.

Well, before this one game, I was riding with Pipe—he was not driving, thankfully—down to Claresholm, and he noticed I was really quiet. I was usually pretty quiet, but on this occasion I was absolutely silent.

So Pipe said, "Something's bothering you, Jim." And after I made him coax me a bit, I proceeded to tell him about Jay Jenkins, this defenceman I mentioned.

I was frustrated. I said to Pipe, "I just can't get by him. I'm embarrassed. I can outskate him but he's such a big guy and such a good defenceman, I'm really beat."

And he said, "Ah, ha..."

"The first problem," he told me, "is in your own mind. You think you can't beat him and that's his best weapon. The rest of the way, while we're driving to Claresholm, think of how well you stickhandle and skate. Right now, start thinking, before we get there"—it was still an hour-and-a-half, two-hour drive away—"I want you to visualize when you get a breakaway, and what you do to fool the goalie, the way you fake to the right, then come back to the left. In your mind. Do that to Jenkins. Pretend he's the goalie."

First time down the ice, I took Pipe's advice. That's exactly what I did. And I dashed around Jay Jenkins like a ballerina! Went through him like a dose of salts.

And Elmer, on my way to the back to the bench, he just kinda nodded at me and smiled. And I thought, *Wow!* That's all it took. That's the kind of guy he was. He had the ability to make you understand ways that you could be better as a player.

Elmer lived here and died here in Okotoks. The Piper family was really well-known around town. A wonderful, wonderful coach, and a great hockey mind.

Just a real good Okotokian. Put it that way.

JOHN DAVIDSON

I like to say I "discovered" John Davidson. All of our scouts at the time with the Centennials, back in juniors, they wouldn't even look at him.

I was running the Scotty Munro Hockey School then. Why me? Well, Scotty told me, "I am looking for hockey players, but the only

reason is so I can hire you and keep you working 'cause you don't have a job in the summer!"

So I did that and they made me sit in their meetings all the time, talking about players.

In one of these meetings, the scouts were giving Scotty names of guys who had impressed them. Well, he got around to me and asked, "Who you got?" And I told him, "I don't understand. There's something very wrong here. Nobody's said a word about the goalie. Tall, skinny drink of water. He's the best gawd-damned guy out there." Nobody at the table said a word.

Everybody's stared at their papers, shuffling 'em.

So Scotty gave me this look and said, "And who might that be?"

And I told him. "Name's John Davidson."

J.D. had signed up for the school. In those days, everybody who did paid their way, $40, but if they were picked to go to training camp later on they got their money back.

So the next day Scotty went out and watched practice, and he came into the meeting room afterward throwing stuff all over the place, hollering, "SOB! What does it say when my trainer's got to come and tell me who the best hockey player we've got out there is?!" And on and on, like that.

He loved John Davidson.

It turned out J.D. got his money back. And look what happened.

GLENN HALL

Goalie. That's what we called Glenn Hall. And he was, as everyone knows, or should, one of the best at the position, ever.

Think of it—he played 502 straight games. Without a mask! Crazy.

Goalie was the goaltending coach of the Flames for awhile. Honestly, it felt like having royalty in the building.

He was great for the team, always boosting everybody's spirits. We were at a charity event once and I was auctioneering. We came to a

framed picture of that famous photo of Bobby Orr flying through the air after scoring the Cup-winning goal for Boston in 1970.

Well, I said, "This is one of the photos we get the most requests for. My hero, Bobby Orr. You have no idea how many times I've auctioned off this picture."

Well, Goalie, he was sitting there, front row—he was the goalie, playing for the Blues, Bobby was flying overtop of after scoring that famous goal, of course—giving me the dirtiest look you can imagine.

We get along great, Glenn and I.

We were on a road trip one time, down east, I think, and everybody from management was there—Cliff Fletcher, Al MacNeil, Al Coates, along with Doug Barkley, all sitting up in the top corner of this rink watching practice. Everybody had grey to white hair.

And Goalie, came over to the bench, leaned against the boards, and nodded up toward the stands.

"Geez, Bear. Look at that. You know what that means? We're going to have to dye our hair white to keep our jobs!"

Bobby was there, too, and we started laughing like three hyenas.

Well, wouldn't you know, we went to L.A. next. We had practice at the Forum and then Bobby and I went for a walk. We were strolling down a street with a couple of stores and one of 'em had a sign in the window: WIGS! ALL ON SALE! I walked maybe three steps and slammed on the brakes. Bobby thought I'd had a heart attack.

I gotta go get a wig.

I walked in and approached this saleslady, told her I needed a grey wig—one that I could cut the hair on easily. They were all women's wigs, so she looked at me funny. But I was so excited. We finally found one that was a little more grey than white.

One of the ladies who worked for the L.A. Kings, up in the bar at the Forum Club, was also a hairdresser. We knew her from there. I found her and told her what I wanted—needed the wig cut, but not too short, like Cliff and Al MacNeil and Coatsey.

199

The game was that night, so I waited until Goalie was there. I put that wig on and walked in where those guys were all talking together, like King Tut from Turd Island.

By now, Bobby was p—ing his pants. Barks was laughing. They all stared at me, started breaking up. I said, "Well, you bastards, Goalie told me I need white hair like you in order stay with this club. How's this?"

Cliff looked at me and said, "You little…" But he smiled when he said it.

Every time Goalie and I talk, to this day, he asks me if I still have that wig.

And I do.

A quiet guy, but he came up with the best stories. And he loves beer. He was asked once at a banquet about playing so much of his career at the old Chicago Stadium. The guy doing the asking said, "Geez, Glenn, that place was so big, 20,000 fans, and so loud it must've driven you nuts." And Glenn tells him, "It was okay. I didn't hear much anyway." The guy then asked him if could hear anything beside a dull roar. He was wondering, you know, if one guy would always be riding him, hollering stuff like, "Hey, Hall, you stink!" or something along those lines.

And Glenn thought on that a bit and said, "Well, there was one particular guy I could hear distinctly." And the guy leaned in to listen better. And Glenn said, "There was this one SOB behind me, in the stands, always yelling, 'Beer! Get your ice-cold beer here!'"

Glenn Hall. I love that man so much.

PHIL RUSSELL

It's kind of weird, but I didn't like Phil Russell at all when he played against us—the Centennials—with the Edmonton Oil Kings. Just a tough, mean potlicker out there on the ice, but for some reason he took to me and befriended me.

When he came over with the Flames from Atlanta it was just a wonderful thing, the same kind of feeling for me as when Lanny arrived.

I just thought the world of Phil Russell.

He used to come down to the Bow River and camp with us. A lot of the players did. I taught them how to fish and things like that. Phil was there all the time.

As a player, he was tough. Brought up that way. With the Oil Kings, of course, he was brought up by Wild Bill Hunter.

Rusty was the instigator of the whole Hawaii thing that first year with Nelson Skalbania—or the Grocery Man, as I called him. Skalbania was the guy who initially snuck in and bought the team out from underneath Doc and B.J. Seaman and those guys.

Skalbania was in the room during the playoffs that first season, talking, like usual, telling everybody how great we were, how well we're playing.

Well, Phil got up and hollered, "Hey, Nelson, if you think we're so damned good why don't you send us all to Hawaii?"

Well, Skalbania laughed, walked around a bit, and within 15 minutes or so came back and said, "Russell, you're right! That's a helluva good idea! Done deal!"

So everybody got to go to Hawaii—wives, kids, players. I went with Shirley and the two boys. *Bingo!* Just like that.

Phil was a pretty hard guy to ignore and he had the balls to make an issue with Skalbania, in front of everybody. And it worked.

I don't remember how long Rusty lasted with us—a couple years? But I do know it wasn't long enough.

PHIL RUSSELL
Calgary Flames, 1980–83

Bearcat is a great human being. Wonderful friend. Best thing that happened to us when we came to Calgary. He's comfortable with himself. And real. He's *real*. Nothing phoney about Bearcat. How's that?

I've got a 41-year-old daughter and a nine-year-old daughter. My nine-year-old hasn't met him yet. But I've got a picture of my 41-year-old when

she was young with her hands on Bearcat's bald head and they're both sleeping.

Whole family's wonderful. I knew Grandpa Bearcat.

They say archenemies make the best friends. That's the way it was when I was with the Oil Kings and Bearcat was with the Centennials.

Years later, here we are in Calgary from Atlanta. A bunch of big boys. Eric Vail. Doc Houston. Guy Chouinard. Willi Plett. Wonderful people. I remember vividly someone going into a corner and basically swallowing his tongue. And Bearcat's out there in a New York minute. I don't think he even had a jaw screw. I think he had those tape scissors and, *Boom!* Problem solved.

When we moved, a whole bunch of different things had to happen. Executive relocation, for one. Some realtor jumped in and we'd sell our place in Atlanta and have an opportunity in Calgary. I moved from a little place in Marietta, Georgia, worth $170,000, to Woodlands, out by the golf course in southwest Calgary. And I'm thinking, *How am I gonna do this?* But everybody helped, including Bearcat.

He made all those transitions easier because he always had fun. We were always up to something. When he'd be telling stories about the old days, he'd look over at me and say, "Ah, he's from Edmonton. We don't associate with him."

So here I am, a true Edmonton guy, coming to Calgary and falling in love with the place. And part of the reason was skinny little potlicker. We'd always joke, "The prettiest girls are always in Calgary. Not up in Edmonton. They're Klondikers up there!"

He wasn't just a trainer and saver of people's lives at times in the game. He was your buddy. I've never been so happy as Lanny scoring a goal and Bearcat hugging the Cup that night they won in Montreal.

I was always telling Cliff Fletcher, "Sign Bearcat to a lifetime contract. He's that valuable."

And I meant it.

BOBBY STEWART

Bobby and I worked together for 16 years, then he spent a couple more seasons with the Flames after I retired before moving back to Atlanta to be equipment manager for the Thrashers.

As I've said, Bobby and I were as different as night and day. Maybe that's the reason we got along so good.

You could not find a better friend, a nicer person. Honestly. I dare you to try.

Funny, Bobby was, but super-serious when it came to his job. Very dedicated. Very quiet, usually. Such a hard worker. Back then, it was just him and me on the road, before Allan joined us.

He'd started in the business with Cliff, in Montreal with the junior Canadiens and the Canadiens, helping out Eddy Palchak. He rejoined Cliff in Atlanta after Cliff had gone to St. Louis for awhile, then Cliff brought him here. He knew what a tireless worker Bobby was. Time, hours, they didn't mean anything to Bobby.

And he had the type of personality to get along with anybody.

That first year of the team being in Calgary, I tried to do what I'd always done—which was everything. With the Centennials, I'd sharpened the skates, drove the bus, tended to the injuries. That's how I'd always operated. At first, I interfered with Bobby's work, which was wrong. Bobby, being Bobby, didn't say a word.

But I found out pretty quick that I didn't have to do everything anymore.

Because Bobby was there.

I just backed off, left him alone. Bobby and I knew we both had experience. I could sharpen the skates and help pack equipment, Bobby could help with the medical side of things. If there was a problem, we were there for each other.

We worked together, as I mentioned, for 16 years. We never had any conflict. Ever. Imagine.

He was very proud of his job, of what he did, which was great. And a very religious person. His wife, Sherri, was a flight attendant. He met her during his first stint in Atlanta. Very nice lady.

But, as I mentioned, he was always heavy. Me, I'd be out running, rollerblading, whatever, and our doctor, Terry Groves, would nag at him, "Bobby, you should get out and do some exercise with Bear. I'm worried about you." And he'd be on me about getting in Bobby's ear and I'd say, "Geezus, Terry, I'm trying but he just won't do it."

Bobby would drink a dozen Cokes a day. I'd try to be subtle and try and steer him away from that. Not that we gave a s—t about it; you could drink a hundred thousand gallons. But it's *bad* for you.

When Bobby left for Atlanta the second time, Eric Vail, Train, really helped with that. He was the instigator, told the team there, the Thrashers, "You've gotta get Bobby back." Things weren't going so well for him here with the Flames.

Then, when he first got back to Atlanta, that's when I heard he had diabetes. Lost a toe. Geez. A year or so later we had the trainers' meeting, in Florida, I think. Bobby was there, skinnier'n a rail. So thin I hardly knew him. At first I thought he was sick but he'd started working out, changing his lifestyle and his diet after he found out about the diabetes.

Then he lost his job when the team moved to Winnipeg, and he wound up at Disney World—his son got him that job. He really enjoyed it there, from what I heard, and was doing fine.

But the damn diabetes got him. He just didn't take care of himself and, like I said, he drank way too much Coke.

When I heard he'd passed in early May 2019, at 69…I mean, it didn't surprise me. I knew in the long run that it would happen, but it broke my heart. He was my partner, my sidekick.

We were a team within the team.

CLIFF FLETCHER

Cliff was the sergeant major of the group. I was kind of afraid of him, but he built that group from a bunch of individuals into a family. A real family. Over the years, he threw a few parties for the whole team at his place in Mount Royal before he moved out to Springbank, where Lanny lives, and they were wonderful.

He was a great guy, and really good with the players. But he was in charge, he had the final decision on everything, so he could be stern if he needed to be. Still, he was a real gentleman and a good boss. He demanded perfection. Even in my job, I had to be on the bit or he'd let me know.

I remember the day he let Terry Crisp go. I get word that Cliff wanted to see me upstairs. So up I went to his office and he told me, "I want to give you some information before it gets out. I had to let Crispie go." And I said, "What the heck?" He gave me his reasons and I just kind of blurted out, "Gawd, didn't he just help us win the Cup?!"

Then he gave me this stare and said, "I didn't bring you up here to ask you if I could let him go. I came up here to tell you I have."

Then I shut up. But he had the courtesy to call me up and tell me himself. That was Cliff. I can't believe the Flames haven't honoured him in some way. He sure deserves it.

I always say that when he went off to Toronto, they should've hired him to run the league. He'd have done a helluva job as commissioner. No idea why nobody talked to him about it.

He understood people. Understood the business. Understood the game, obviously. Classy. He was respected everywhere, by everybody. The ideal man to do that job. Absolutely perfect. I really think they missed the boat on that one.

MIKE VERNON

To me, he was the best goalie we've ever had. Grew up a half-block away from me. His dad, Martin, coached both my boys, Allan and Danny, in baseball and in hockey.

So I know the family really well.

I still remember getting out of the house in the morning to leave for the Saddledome, hopping in the car, and I had that half-block to reach the end of the street. And there'd be Mikey going to school. He'd get halfway out into the crosswalk, wave, and yell, "Hi, Mr. Murray!"

Pret'near every day that happened.

And then to think not that long later we'd be working together and winning a Stanley Cup together…isn't that something? What are the odds?

Even as a kid he was an arrogant little potlicker. I guess he had to be. His dad was the same way. Good guys, but full of confidence.

He was always solid in goal, a star from peewee on up through juniors, and the whole neighbourhood let him know it. Mike grew up that way, getting a lot of attention.

I understand the small-guy thing, being one myself. He always felt he had to prove himself, and that's what he did.

The year we won the Cup he meant a lot. So much.

And watching replays of the games since then, I believe that more than ever. Just thinking about the saves he made on Stan Smyl in Game 7 of the first round versus Vancouver still makes me shudder.

Mikey might let in a bad one—guys used to kid him about that—but then he'd shut the door. When it mattered, he was there.

I don't think he ever received the attention he deserved. Not like Grant Fuhr or Patrick Roy. It might've had something to do with his attitude. And his being a local guy. I also don't think a lot of people here forgave him for the year ('83) the Wranglers—I was with the Flames by then but Allan was working for the Wranglers—should've won the Memorial Cup but were beaten out by Lethbridge, and then rather than

join Lethbridge after that he went to play for Portland, and they ended up winning the tournament!

It didn't bother me. I knew him the way I knew my own kids.

As a goalie, he was just so quick, so agile on his feet. They didn't wear all the equipment they do today so he had to be really athletic, even more so because of his size.

He didn't play deep a lot, just stayed in the net and did his thing. Always looked after himself, was always near the top in the physical testing, even when he reached the Flames.

Another thing about Mikey was: he took a lot of punishment. Looking back, it amazes me. I was his trainer so it really bothered me. Players would run him behind the net, in front of the net, beside the net, and get away with it all the time. The referees didn't do a damn thing!

Poor old Mike would get blasted by someone but he didn't respond. He also didn't try to get out of the way and be chickens—t about it, no matter what. He stood in there, didn't let it throw him off his game.

Maybe they were trying to wind him up. I don't know. But he refused to take the bait. It used to p—s me off how many times he'd get hit. And if it got me mad, I can't imagine how he felt.

I'd see him go down after getting knocked on his butt, again, and think, *Oh, geez, he's gotta be hurt.* But he'd be bounce right back up. Tough little potlicker, in his way.

Should he be in the Hall of Fame? I think so. You look at what he's done, winning Cups on two different teams and a Conn Smythe Trophy as playoff MVP. That's a pretty good resume for anyone, in my opinion.

I think he was awesome. Just an awesome goalie. And I'd say the same thing even if he hadn't grown up half a block away from me.

MIKE VERNON
Calgary Flames, 1986–94, 2000–02

The Bearcat story everybody remembers involving me is that time in the playoffs when Bernie Nicholls punched me in the face.

No penalty, naturally. You could get away with that stuff back then—as long as the penalties were even by the end of the night.

So Bearcat thought I was really hurt, came scampering out onto the ice, and the play continued. When he was out there, we scored. He leaned over me, asking, really concerned, "Vernie, Vernie, you all right!?" I told him, "Yeah, Bear, I was just trying to draw a penalty." And he was like, "Oh, am I ever in s—t! We just scored. They're gonna call the goal back." I was like, "Geez, I hope not. Okay, let's just sit here and see what happens. I'll just milk it some more."

That's how I remember the conversation.

Meanwhile, Gretzky was after the ref, losing his marbles. It was hil-arious.

Bearcat did it all. We used to get our legs rubbed and it was like "For f—k's sake, Bear, put on some gloves!" Those old, gnarled hands of his…it was like having your legs rubbed with 120 sandpaper.

I remember Joe Nieuwendyk coming into the dressing room and putting on David Wilcox singing that song "Do the Bearcat." That's the way it was back then. The guy was a social butterfly. He loved everybody, took care of everybody. That's just his nature.

Bottom line: he'd do anything to win; make sure that everything was good and that you were ready to go for the game.

He was always there for you. If I hadn't had a good game, knew I wasn't happy, was maybe dragging my a— a bit, he'd say, "Vernie, come into my office." Then we'd sit, have a beer, and talk. He had a knack for making you feel better. And not just on the training side of things.

I've known Bearcat a long time. When I was eight years old, he lived around the corner from me. I knew his sons, AlCat and Danny, who was

the same age as me. I knew he was the trainer for the Centennials, the Cowboys with Don "Smokey" McLeod in goal, then the Flames.

I mean, everybody knew the guy. He was a big deal when I was a kid. Still is.

BRIAN SPENCER

Brian came in to play for the Centennials after Scotty had scouted him up in Fort St. James.

We were his landlords. Brian, and three other guys, lived at our place. Shirley thought the world of him. She loved him.

But he was a complete nut.

I've got to say he behaved himself when he was here. At least that I know of. He was sort of arrogant and half-a—ed uncontrollable, but Papke liked him because he was a tough kid. And he played hard. Really hard. No different than Lanny McDonald.

All the trouble started after he was drafted by Toronto, then went to Buffalo. That's where he got the name Spinner, in Buffalo, because he was taking drugs.

When he was with us he was just go, go, go. He'd get up, walk on his hands, close them into fists, right out the front door, down the steps, and out to the street when he was going to high school.

He was a fitness nut. At night we'd hear him—he was in the room next to us—huffing and puffing and Shirley would say, "What's the matter with Brian?" I'd tell her, "Don't worry, Shirley, he's just doing push-ups."

He was just completely crazy about hockey, obsessed with getting to the NHL and the Toronto Maple Leafs. It was do-or-die for him.

His dad was just as nuts as Brian. He was so excited that his son was going to make his NHL debut with the Toronto Maple Leafs— remember, that's when they were telecasting the Vancouver game—the

209

guy drove a long ways to a TV station with a friggin' gun, bashing on the door.

Well, they got scared, called the cops, and *boom*. Shot him dead.

We saw Brian from time to time after he reached the NHL. He'd come to visit in the summer, stay two or three days, once with this damned car that took up two thirds of the block when he parked in front of our house. Then he got into the motorcycles, and he showed up with this motorcycle so damn big we had to put it corner-ways in my backyard. Like the one Peter Fonda rode in the movie *Easy Rider*. Brian had copied that. And then he took off, the potlicker, leaving it there, corner-to-corner in the backyard. I was just scared somebody was going to come and try and steal it.

He ended up retired in Florida, a drug dealer, and some guy put a bullet in his head. That was it. When I heard, I was so sad but not surprised. I'd known for a long time that he was in trouble. The way it played out was tough because we both, Shirley and I, really liked him. He was a genuinely likeable guy.

But you could tell it was going to be a one-way ticket, even when he was a kid.

DANNY GARE

I know I talk a lot about Danny Gare, but that's because I love the guy.

In juniors I was the Man of Many Hats, of course. One of those hats was the bus driver's. One time we were going up to Flin Flon but Scotty figured we didn't have time to get there because the previous night we were playing in Prince Albert. So he proposed that we leave the bus there, in the barn of a friend of his, fly to Flin Flon, and then fly back, get the bus, and he'd have it sitting there at the airfield, running, warm and ready to go when everybody got off the plane.

Well, we got back from Flin Flon and...no bus. Of course.

I was frantic, got on the phone. Eventually, the guy showed up and we loaded up the bus. It was the middle of the night, cold, snowing,

and we had to get back to Calgary because we just played the last game before Christmas and the kids were all going home.

Danny Gare was going back to B.C.; other guys were fanning out all over the place. But it was always gonna be a close shave getting back in time for Danny's plane.

Anyway, I started thinking, *I'm not gonna let Danny down!*

But I was tired. Just beat. And it's a nine- to 10-hour drive, right? On top of that, the snow was getting so bad that this one kid on the team, tall guy with long arms, he'd be reaching around me while I was leaning, my arms around the steering wheel, and scraping the ice off the windshield for me!

Anyway, we got home—I'm amazed, looking back, that we actually made it to where we were headed half the time, that we never had a really bad accident.

If we did that nowadays we'd probably all go to jail.

And Danny made his flight! Those kids, all of 'em, were so appreciative of what I'd done. To this day, they remember that situation.

I cared about each and every one of those kids. But Danny, maybe a little bit more.

Wonderful family, mom and dad and his brother. He came from a family of athletes, was brought up that way.

With him, doing the right thing was just automatic. He'd take on anybody. Of course, he got that reputation while he played in Buffalo, but those of us with the Centennials at the time could've told them.

They loved him in Buffalo same as Calgary loved him when he played junior here.

I know one thing—if we'd have had him with the Flames for all those games against Edmonton, he'd have kicked their a—. Every one of them. No fear.

Nothing intimidated him.

Just that type of guy.

211

TERRY CRISP

I really enjoyed Crispie. We had so much fun with him, always laughing and joking. But on the bench he was crazy. A real cheerleader. Running up and down, yelling and hollering. So full of energy. Just a bull.

Poor Bobby Stewart was always in the way and Crispie'd be yelling at him, "Get the hell out of the way, Bobby!"

We were both afraid we might get hurt.

Bobby would be dodging out the way the whole game, trying to avoid getting run over by Crispie.

During the game he'd be super serious, but there was always this playful side to him too. How about the time during that Chicago series in '89 when we scored in OT, then he scaled the glass and kissed Al MacNeil's wife instead of his own wife, Sheila, by mistake?

That's him. So gung-ho. Spontaneous.

You know, I don't think Crispie received near as much credit as he deserved the year we won the Cup.

Things had been kinda haywire at that time, coming off the Badger days. Yes, we had a real good team, loads of skill and grit, but sometimes it isn't easy coaching a deep, talented team; keeping everybody happy.

We win two Presidents' Trophies and the Stanley Cup in what, three years he was here, and then he gets fired?

Kinda weird. I honestly think with Crispie at the helm we win a couple more times. But that's just my view.

HARLEY AND DOC

That original ownership group were all wonderful, wonderful people; that's no secret. But Harley Hotchkiss and Doc Seaman ran the team.

What you saw was them.

Doc was a cowboy, an oil man, a rancher, and a better talker than Harley. Just a really, really good person. Harley was the same, only quiet, very unassuming.

His wife, Becky, was a lovely lady.

Harley and Doc, a real Mutt and Jeff situation.

They catered to the employees—*all* the employees, down to the stick boys, the guy at the back door. They knew everybody's name, took time to talk to people, you betcha. That counts for plenty. No detail was too small.

They carried that franchise, the two of them. So different as people but such good friends. Harley was trusted by everybody—by players, agents, personnel, you name it. A good businessman and an honest, sincere person. You could take his word at face value.

You run into so many shysters and a—holes, you try your best, work your a— off, and suddenly somebody's reading you the riot act and you can't understand why. Just because they can, I guess, or it makes them feel superior.

Harley and Doc, those guys were a dream. No fear involved with them. Good, pleasant people who respected what you did and both had the organization at heart.

They treated us like *we* owned the business and they were just working there. They ran this team the way all the other teams wanted to be run, should've been run, or should be run.

Everybody loved them and they loved everyone.

AL MACNEIL

As I mentioned, when I went to New York and worked with the Rangers that one playoff year, the word was already out that the Flames would be moving from Atlanta to Calgary.

I've talked about me talking to Cliff Fletcher, the story about Atlanta's trainer showing up and deciding he had no use for the Corral, all that history.

Well, after the first time I'd spoken with Cliff, he told me the coach—who'd been with the team in Atlanta—would be coming in this one afternoon at such-and-such time, and I'd better go over to the hotel he'd

be staying at and introduce myself. Hadn't gotten the job yet. Didn't seem likely to. But that it wouldn't hurt.

Besides, I'd never met Al MacNeil before.

Anyway, I approached Al in the lobby of the hotel after he arrived and told him who I was, and he kinda hemmed and hawed. "Okay…. Yeah…" In other words: B—er off. Leastwise, it sounded that way to me.

But then he said, "Glad to meet you."

Later, after the crap hit the fan with Norm Mackie and Cliff realized he was probably going to be stuck with me, he told me I'd better scoot along and talk to Al again.

I remember being very, very cautious and nervous about seeing Al. Well, at that time he had no interest in making a hit with me. So it was very dicey, touch-and-go, I thought, whether I'd get the job or not.

I had no idea at that moment what a great guy he was, is, not until I had the opportunity to work with him day-to-day that first season and then over the years.

Al is a gentleman. That's the best way I can describe him. And that's a pretty important thing to be able to say about anybody, I think.

He'd had some tough times while coaching in Montreal—where he led them to a Stanley Cup, don't forget—particularly when he was out in the Maritimes with the Nova Scotia Voyageurs down east in the minors. Took a s—t-kicking there, but he did a great job with us.

Remember, that wasn't an easy group to coach.

Al proved to be very quiet on the ice during practice. He had played a long time in the league, so he was very experienced.

Then, of course, after he stopped coaching following our first year in Calgary, he stayed onboard in a number of management positions and got to be a really good friend. Al became Cliff's right-hand man and that made sense; they were a lot alike. Cliff was the one who made us like a family and Al carried on that approach forever, even after Cliff left. They trusted each other, respected each other's opinion.

That's the Montreal influence, eh?

Al always treated me wonderfully well. To this day, he calls me "Pal." *Hiya Pal, how are ya?* Like that. As if Pal had been printed on my birth certificate. That sticks with me.

His wife, Norma, is such a sweetheart. Lovely lady, whom everybody remembers Crispie scaling the glass to kiss after we'd won that overtime game in Chicago on the way to the Cup.

She was forever kidding me about getting all the ink that I received in the papers, attention on the radio, wherever. Which I guess I did from time to time, for whatever reason. Al was, as I said, a quiet, stay-out-of-the-spotlight type of guy.

Her joking was all in fun, though.

If we were at a party or a function somewhere, she'd come in, come over, and kiss my hand, real formal, as if she was kissing the Pope's ring. Always, always jabbing me that way. I got a kick out of it. Kind of a running gag between us.

I used to see her on the driving range out at Heritage Pointe, hitting golf balls, and she'd do the very same thing! All pomp and circumstance, she'd waltz over and kiss my hand.

We had such great people everywhere you looked in the organization in those days. So good. *So* good. And Al was a big part of all that.

I think the world of him.

As I said, a real gentleman.

SHELDON KENNEDY

I first met Sheldon through Theo Fleury. That's when Sheldon was playing for Swift Current, for that dirty coach, Graham James.

Theo was with us by that time. Swift Current came into town one time and he introduced me to Sheldon and said, "Bear, can you help him out? He's playing very well for that team but he's got no equipment. His equipment is crap." So I said, "Hell, yeah." Then I went to Bobby and we lined him up—shin pads, shoulder pads, everything. Well, Sheldon was just flabbergasted. Little did we know that was when

he was going through the abuse by his coach. But he sure seemed to be a nice kid.

All of a sudden, a few years later, he showed up on our team. We still didn't know what the root of the problem was when he came and played for us, but at the time he was a drinker. He was tested every day. No problem. Never once did he blow any number. Zero, always.

He was never a problem or even bitched. "Okay, Bear. Let's get 'er done."

Just a really good guy. But you could tell he was having problems, even when he was with us. We just didn't know why.

It's a damned shame it took that long for what he went through to come to light. Now it doesn't stay silent long because people are paying attention. Back then, nobody paid attention. And they didn't give a s—t. They didn't want any problems, didn't want to create any problems, so they chose to stay away from it, as far as I'm concerned.

That whole ugly experience was one of those things that Sheldon buried in his heart and in his head. What he went through must've been unbelievable.

You see him today and shoot, I'm just so proud of him. Speaking out, being a voice for people who have problems through no fault of their own. He owned a place near us, bought a ranch, let my sons Danny and Allan camp down there. We got involved with AA, helping out, and it's been great.

I went partway with him that time he rollerbladed from Edmonton to Calgary. I met up with him near Airdrie—someone drove me down there—and rollerbladed the rest of the way into town beside him. Darn near killed myself. I was an old fart. But I was very proud of being able to do that with him.

God-darn, what he's done is just outstanding.

THE FRATERNITY

TRAINERS, I'M PROUD TO SAY, are a special breed. We stick together. We're in this together, looking after our players.

Back in the day, I'd get on the phone and call, say, Pete Demers in L.A. or Tom Woodcock in San Jose. I could call any of them, on any team, and say, "Geezus, you guys, I've got a problem with a player whose back is getting cross-checked all the time," and they would talk to me about similar injuries they'd dealt with, what kind of treatments or medicines they'd used.

They'd tell me to phone their team doctors, give me the numbers—I knew the doctors all because we'd make sure when we went into a city we made a big effort to get to know them, because we needed them on our side.

And they all were great, digging through records and things to help out in any way they could. We were doing that sort of thing all the time.

We didn't care what team a guy played for. I mean, I was back and forth on the phone with the guys in Edmonton often, and they were our biggest rival.

We wanted all the guys healthy. So I'd call the trainers and they'd call me.

Sometimes, a trainer would call and say, "What the hell did you do in this case?" And I may not have dealt with it in hockey, but I had in

football, while I was working with the Stampeders, alongside Alec, and this is what we did. Or maybe I'd come across the same sort of problem during my rodeo days.

We were always, always, honest with each other, no matter what. You trusted these people. There were two or three guys on every team—*every* team, mind—that you could positively count on to help you. I even called opposition teams' doctors for advice. No problem.

An example of the communication and cooperation between everybody: Lanny McDonald and Doug Risebrough were dealing with these awful groin/hip flexor problems at one time. Sometimes bad enough that they couldn't play. So I called Demers in L.A. and he lined me up with the trainer for the Olympic cyclists, someone who'd dealt with a lot of these types of issues. I talked to the guy and he was very pleased I'd called. I told him, "Well, you're the guy that knows." He explained to me with the cyclists they'd go out and train and train and train, all bent over, for hours. So you've got to stretch the s—t out of them. More so for that than for hockey, dealing with skating; because of the position, the muscles tighten up and tear.

So the cyclists did an incredible amount of stretching exercises. When I heard this, I thought, "I'll be a SOB, that's the same thing that happens to bronc riders," who I worked with in the summertime.

Well, I got Lanny and Riser onto this stretching regimen, and I'd be there doing yoga with them.

Lanny, in particular, improved like hell. But the point is: I was able to help because of Pete, his advice, and the network we had set up.

Pete Demers, we all owe him so much. He's the reason I have a pension today. He pushed for that and finally the NHL agreed. A great friend. To all of us.

PETE DEMERS
L.A. Kings trainer, 1972–2006

Bearcat is one-of-a-kind, for sure. What you see is what you get.

We're a family. In those early years, we were trying to build our association up so the sense of camaraderie was very strong. We were there to improve our professionalism, but the game is about the players, not about the trainers, so in a lot of cases it's an uphill battle. We had a lot of resistance in getting good equipment. We had one bike and they hung their clothes on it. We had one set of dumbbells and they used them to hold the door open.

Then you see what they have today and it's amazing. Guys like Bearcat pushed for improvements for the betterment of the game.

Oh, yeah, I remember him running on the ice against us while the play was going on. I don't remember a lot of the details, but I do remember him, plain as day, going out to the right of the bench.

The reason he did is that, play or no play, he saw that his player was down and he needs help. That just shows you the character and credibility of Bearcat.

He's a celebrity in Calgary. The recognition that he's given our group, the support people—trainers, equipment managers, staff—has really helped.

He's been a great representative for our profession and a great ambassador for the game.

The teams may have been competing. We, the trainers, weren't competing. As I said, we were, every one of us, guys who cared about the players. All players.

Woody in San Jose. Tremendous. We became pals. I called him a lot about Joe Nieuwendyk and Gary Roberts and their back problems. He'd hunt around and call me a week or 10 days later: "Bear, I just ran into a friend of mine at such-and-such college," and he'd tell me the advice that guy had given him on backs.

Everybody was only too glad to help each other.

In this job, you were always dealing with different problems. I got along great with all our doctors. Terry Groves, Lowell Van Zuiden. All those guys.

We worked together...the doctors, the ambulance people, everybody. Because we all had the players' best interests at heart. A common cause.

Gary Suter, one time, rang me up in middle of the night, 2 AM. He called from home, really hurting. Thought he had appendicitis. He explained it all to me, handed the phone to his wife, and I told her, "Call an ambulance. Get Gary to the Holy Cross Hospital. Right away." So I contacted our doctor, Terry, and he contacted the right people, specialists, and we all reached the hospital before Sutes. Turned out he needed major surgery. An emergency operation. They removed his appendix. And we'd had no indication before he called me.

You can't p—s around. So you make sure the right people, the top guys in their fields, are there. We had such a big array of specialists, for MRIs and things of that nature. *Boom!* Done. Everyone schooled me.

They were my professors.

TERRY GROVES
Calgary Flames doctor, 1980–2003

Bearcat saved my behind I don't know how many times. He really did. Because he knew these guys, when they weren't right. For instance, in the early concussion days he'd evaluate the guy as soon as he got back on the ice and he'd be able to realize the guy wasn't right. If I followed his advice, all was good. If I didn't, it wasn't.

I learned very quickly that Bearcat knew more about concussions than most doctors did at that time.

He knew when a guy had a ding and whether it was important or wasn't. He was way ahead of us in that area. Bearcat was someone other trainers around the league would go to for advice.

Doctors are flies on the wall, as if we're not there. I remember Crispie coming into the dressing room one day, saying, "This is what we're going to do. This is how we're going to press them." And as soon as left, you heard of a chorus of, "We're not going to do that." So we heard a lot. And it didn't take long to understand the respect Bearcat commanded.

Guys didn't want to miss shifts, let alone games, so Bearcat had to be on top of his game, to explain to the player that this knee or that elbow wasn't right, let's get it right.

He was the best doctor we had for the first few years, until I learned.

No one wanted a trainer that was whistling or waffling about things. Bearcat didn't. He was dang sure what was going on because he'd played a lot of hockey and understood what was important and what wasn't. We were really dependent on him a lot of times. The players really trusted him; he'd quiet them down a lot. After practices or warm-up, you'd always hear, "Bearcat! Bearcat! I need you!" They didn't call for the doctors. They called for Bearcat.

A couple of times we had a coach or two who didn't want players out of the lineup but Bearcat would say, "He can't play." And he was always right. We didn't take any chances when Bearcat said no. That was the level of trust we had with him. Boy, did he care. Those guys were his kids. They were not hockey players, they were his boys.

So he was always on the side of health, making sure they were safe.

He'd give advice on vitamins and things like that. I remember one time he did make a mistake, putting a big bowl of vitamins out, niacin, and the coach grabbed a whole handful of these things. And what they made you do, if you took them on an empty stomach you'd get severe flushes. Well, the coach got terribly flushed and thought he was going to die.

So we didn't do that any more.

Alec Recsky, my mentor, would always tell me to watch those people, study them, and learn what I could. I was receiving an education

not many people could get. And they learned a lot from me, which is something I wasn't aware of until later, when they told me.

Most of the time you were dealing with cuts to the face. I remember Lowell Van Zuiden telling me, "I don't know why I'm doing the sutures. You know more than me. I watched you darn socks, you do a helluva job!" That's the one thing the guys were always leery about—scars. Don't leave a scar.

Frank Musil, for instance, would not take freezing. He hated the needles. So he'd sit there and take the stitches with no freezing. No sweat. But the needle? No way.

Killer, Doug Gilmour, was the same. "Just sew me up!" he'd say. "Give me a whiskey in a dirty glass and sew me up!"

LOWELL VAN ZUIDEN
Calgary Flames doctor, 1986–95

The thing that sticks in my mind is the respect the players had for him. You must remember that office in the back, behind the trainers' room and beside the dressing room? That was kind of a refuge for the players. How many people came in there and kicked that bucket in there, then they'd slink off into Bear's office. You'd see them sitting there with their Father Confessor. That was so important for the players. His office was a place they could separate themselves from whatever pressures were coming down from above.

I'll never forget the day Kent Nilsson walked into the dressing room with these alligator-skin shoes on. And Bear's staring at him, like, "My god, *where* did you get those things?!"

You also never knew what was in his trunk when we went on the road.

Everybody was a fan of Bear's. That was the big thing. Just his personality—such a likeable guy. When we went to the Soviet Union and Czechoslovakia, for instance, the massage guy we had in Czech *loved* Bear.

I can remember we had some physios come in, but the players would always go ask, "What do you think I should do, Bear?"

From my perspective, same thing—I trusted him.

And it wasn't like he gave the sense that he knew everything. He knew what he knew, knew what he didn't, and knew how to deal with that. He understood the psychology of the players enough to earn their trust.

He knew when he was outside of his area of expertise, and it didn't bother him. He knew when he needed help. On that score, Bear was 100 per cent. That was important.

There was a huge transition that took place in the, oh, I want to say late '80s: when the *Playboy* magazines came out of the toilets in the dressing room and the contract book went in. Something changed. And the contract book would be in there, with all the stats, and they'd be studying it inside-out.

And Bear understood that, too. He understood that seismic shift.

This, the willingness of fellow trainers to help, extends all the way back to my days in juniors. The guy in Regina, the guy in Lethbridge, the guy in Flin Flon. You name it.

Amazing, the things you come to know. And if you needed help, people were always coming out of the woodwork, ready. Same as today.

What a wonderful profession.

Yeah, in this job you're out on the road a lot. I spent so much time shuttling around. But it didn't seem like any sort of sacrifice. Because every stop we'd make, I had the chance to see old friends, talk, tell stories, share information.

To this day, we keep in touch, all the trainers from back in the day. I'm on Facebook, discussing things with them. We have a trainer's society. The new guys are on there, of course, but the old guys, the retired guys, are there, too. Still talking. Still learning. Still interested.

FAMILY

A JOB LIKE MINE, well, it's tough on the family. You're away from home a lot, at least during the winter, and the hours are long.

Shirley, when she first met me, when we started going together, well, thank god for her or none of this ever would've happened. I met her in Estevan when I was working for Oil Well Supply.

Best thing that ever happened to me.

She says she never liked me back then at first, always fightin' when I played hockey. But hell, I was just trying to save my life, being a little guy. And I must've had something for her, right?

Shirley and I weren't *together* then, but everywhere we went, the other one seemed to be around. A big group of us would hang around.

She'd lost her mother, and her dad—stepdad, actually—worked in the oil patch as a land man.

Jimmy Dahl, a friend of mine, would always kid me about Shirley, give me a bad time, and I guess he finally badgered us into being a couple. So I owe Jimmy, big time.

Shirley's the reason that I was able to become a trainer, that we took the path that we did, that I even had a chance at the life I got to enjoy.

I remember sitting at her grandmother's table, giving her the news that I'd just gotten a message from Oil Well Supply telling me I was

being sent somewhere I'd never heard of—Podunk Junction, west of Edmonton, I think it was.

Anyway, somewhere so far out in the bush that it'd take 'em a week to find us.

She was sitting there, tears in her eyes. And I told her, "There's only one thing that can maybe happen to stop this." She asked, "What's that?"

"Well, if we get married."

She kinda blinked. "What would that do?"

And I told her, "I'd say to hell with them and take the job I've been offered here. That's the deal. You marry me and I'm staying put."

That set the whole chain of events in motion.

Even then, after we got married, I was in the oil patch and was on the road 24 hours a day, forever, it seemed like. The oil was really booming at that time. So I was away all the time. Not necessarily far away, but there were days and days where I couldn't get home. And in those times, remember, we had to find a pay phone at some garage to even call back home.

She got kinda used to that, so when I switched into the hockey business, which also meant being away a lot and long hours, she was prepared.

While I was trainer for the Centennials, Scotty Munro told me, "If I'm gonna pay you year round, you've got to get your a— out here in the summertime." So I ended up running the hockey school as the manager.

Well, I'd come home and everybody, all these kids, had jerseys. And Shirley'd wash 'em every day, hang them on the clothesline behind the house to dry. All the neighbours thought she was running a laundry service out of the house!

We had our kids at home, of course, but we also took on boarders, three of the Centennials—Jimmy Watson, who played 10 years for Philadelphia, Spinner Spencer, others—and she also babysat three kids from Okotoks during the day. They'd go to school with our sons. So she looked after them.

230

Then one of my brothers, Norman, wound up staying with us, too, going to school, SAIT, studying to be an engineer.

So we had a house full of people.

And one bathroom.

But we got through it, no ruckus, and that was all Shirley. Imagine, a girl who grew up living with her grandmother, mother gone, stepdad a—hole, it's amazing what she's done. And then getting tangled up with me, a little potlicker changing jobs and getting into the type of business I did, it's just amazing.

ALLAN MURRAY
Assistant trainer, Calgary Centennials, Calgary Cowboys, Calgary Wranglers, Calgary Flames; Bearcat's son

Him and my mom, they're just people magnets. The amount of friends they have blows me away. Dad has a way of making people feel important. And he could talk to anybody.

We'd go down to L.A. and the movie stars or TV stars he knew, I could never get over that. He got to know Jamie Farr, for instance. One time Jamie Farr came to Calgary and we went golfing with him. Another time he told me—this is the next day—that he'd been walking through the lobby in the hotel in L.A. and some guy had been stumbling around so he'd helped him and they struck up a conversation going up on the elevator. Dad said, "I think he's kind of famous." And I said, "Did you get his name?"

And Dad said, "Yeah. Said his name is Billy Joel." Dad had no idea who he was.

What impresses me most about him? Well, his work ethic. And his care for people. I mean, with the Centennials he did the job of 10 people. He drove the bus. He did the laundry. He cleaned the dressing room. He helped the players. He ordered the meals and the hotels. Nowadays, they have a person for each one of those jobs.

For the longest time it was just Dad and Bobby on the road. Then I finally got onboard and the three of us were still swamped with work. I honestly don't know how the two of them did it.

There were 17–18 hours days but we didn't think anything of it. We'd sleep in the dressing room most of the time.

We had such a great group in those days, we didn't mind doing all the extras we could for these guys.

There were scary moments. That time in Minnesota, at the old Met Centre, when the puck hit Dad in the eye. He went down like a shot and he was yelling, "My eye! My eye!" I don't know where we were headed the next day to play but he had to stay over, eventually went home.

But he was lucky. Almost lost the eye.

One time when I was working with the Wranglers, Dad got sick and couldn't go on the road with the Flames to L.A. So he convinced Doug Sauter to let me go in his place. Needless to say, I was pretty nervous. The game starts—it was a TV game—and I was thinking, *Please, please, let's just get through this with nobody getting hurt.* Third period, sure enough, Lanny went down. And I was like, "Oh, no..."

So I went running out there. He was hurt but playing it down. I was asking him, "Lanny, Lanny, what's going on? What's the matter?"

And as he was getting up he said, "I'm okay. I just wanted to get you on TV."

Kinda like Dad, I guess.

The wives of hockey players, hockey trainers, anybody involved in the game, don't get near enough credit. Shirley kept everything together at home. All the wives of the players—Ardell McDonald and all them—just loved her. She was in that group. Still is.

Allan, of course, went into the training side of things. Why, I have no idea.

He's five years older than Danny, at the right age, I guess. I just thought it was great that he showed an interest.

I'd taught him to sharpen skates before, so he was in like Flynn there. Same way my dad had taught me when I was 10 years old. I'd sharpen the skates for all the kids in town at the elevator where he worked back in the day.

Allan just kind of tagged along, everyone took a liking to him, and so we hired him.

Then he took to the medical end of it, as well. He followed me when I'd go to work with the Stampeders, for all the home games as well as the practices.

He really started with the Centennials. Then, when Joe Crozier arrived in charge of the WHA Cowboys, he grabbed Allan and gave him a contract. He told me, "He's awesome!" At 16 years old, a pro contract—isn't that quite something?—to be the assistant trainer.

Allan took off a couple of years to work in the oil patch, up in Grande Prairie, but then he came back, went with the Wranglers, and then joined me on the Flames.

He was my son but I was tough on him, no favourites, gave him hell when I thought it was necessary. Looking back, maybe I was too tough. I'd give him s—t and that bothers me now. I think I'd be different today, but I suppose people say that all the time, don't they?

Sometimes it was because I thought I was doing something wrong and I'd take it out on him. You tend to be tougher on your own son, for whatever reason, than you would somebody else's son.

The truth is, Allan got to be a really good trainer and helped me so much. I trusted him, so did the players, and in this business if you don't have that sort of trust everything falls apart. A lot of times he'd notice something wrong with a player before I did and tell me about it. No problem. An ideal situation, as far as I was concerned.

When I left the juniors to go to the Flames, Allan stayed one season as head trainer of the Wranglers and then moved up to join me. Allan

can be a quiet guy, but I remember in the WHA, being in Winnipeg—they were awful, chirping at him all the time—and him getting into a fight with one of the fans, a guy beside the bench. Joe Crozier was on me: "Bear! Get that kid down to the other side of the bench!" But Allan just had enough and wasn't going to take anymore.

We worked a lot together, for different teams in different leagues and different sports. So to eventually win a Stanley Cup with him there alongside me, the feeling…you have no idea. Made me so proud.

Just absolutely outstanding, to have him there, as well as my dad. My dad was still alive then and in Montreal the night we won.

My dad had been the whole reason I'd gotten into hockey in the first place. The name, Bearcat, came from hockey. Everything came from hockey. We had season tickets at the Corral and Saddledome, of course, and Shirley and he would sit together, during the Centennials days and the Cowboys days and the Flames, of course.

The whole fam-damly was big into hockey.

That's the reason I was quite surprised that Danny didn't take to the life the same way. He tried it. Didn't like it. I received a handwritten letter from him after one road trip, I think. Still have the thing. "I can no longer work for my dad," he wrote.

I was dumbfounded when he quit.

For a long time I felt bad, figured maybe I'd been too hard on him too. But looking back, I don't think so. No harder than I was with Allan.

Some people just take a liking to it as a career, and some don't, I guess.

I'm so proud of Danny because he just went off and did his own thing. He attended high school, then went to SAIT, then a job with the city, and every time he applied for something new he got it. *Boom!* He had his engineering ticket, looked after the arenas and the swimming pools. He also worked in the Saddledome for a while, as an assistant engineer. Nothing to do with the Flames but with the building.

Through that, he ended up with the fire department, as a civilian, did a helluva job there, and then the YMCA came after him and now he's a vice president.

Everything Danny did, he did on his own. Allan and I were always off with the hockey team. He went his own way and he was right.

You know, looking back, I've been extremely lucky when it comes to my family. And I'm thankful for them every day.

DANNY MURRAY
Bearcat's son

I'm often asked why I didn't follow in my father's footsteps.

Well, way back in the '70s, he actually did offer me a job working with him, to see if I'd like to get into training, the way he had. I figured I'd give it a try.

I recall being on a trip to Billings with the junior Calgary Wranglers. After getting there the night before the game, I was helping Dad monitor the players for whatever they needed, keeping them in their rooms for curfew. A difficult assignment when you're talking about players like Kelly Kisio, Warren Skorodensky, Ray Cote, causing mischief.

There were water fights in the hotel rooms, etc., and at one point I found Dad outside. The players were using bedsheets tied together to try and escape out windows late at night.

He knew all their tricks.

On game day, working the gate on the bench you had to have your head on your shoulders to make sure there weren't too many players on the ice. You had to be quick to replace a broken stick or damaged piece of equipment.

I'd also hold a flashlight as Dad applied stitches to an injured eye, or stitched back on a piece of ear or part of a nose, etc.

Bench-clearing brawls were pretty common back then, so another responsibility was collecting gear on the ice, sometimes even while the fighting was going on.

I decided that life just wasn't for me. I guess I just wanted to be a player on the ice more than being on the sidelines. So on the seven-plus-hour bus ride back home I crafted a resignation letter, not knowing quite how to give it to my dad. I think I left it on the pillow in his hotel room on one trip. I'm sure Dad still gets a kick out of the story and I'm sure he still has that letter, I think even framed on a wall somewhere.

That was the end of my athletic training career.

My brother, Allan, on the other hand, had already really gotten into the hockey trainers' life and loved it. He really succeeded, working with teams like the WHL Wranglers, WHA Cowboys, and then, of course, alongside Dad on the NHL Flames.

I remember in 1989—a very important year for Calgary, of course—it was my 25th birthday and my parents had a party at the old house in Altadore.

Everyone, all the family and my friends, was there except Allan. Couldn't find him anywhere. I figured he must be out somewhere still celebrating the Stanley Cup win and had missed his little brother's party.

Suddenly, he burst in the front door, dragging a large metal chest. This chest was all dented up with foam and straw hanging out, and it looked like it had been dragged behind a truck for a while.

Allan proceeded to put it on the coffee table and said, "Happy birthday, little brother!" I was hesitant to open it, but Dad urged me to go ahead.

When I opened it, there it was. Allan had managed to steal the Stanley Cup!

Now that's a gift not many other little brothers receive. When word got out, the whole neighbourhood came over. The biggest birthday party I ever had!

In a way, I feel I did follow in my father's footsteps. Through his example, I learned to take in stride whatever the situation was at hand, to make the best of it and, most importantly, to enjoy the journey along the way.

Do that, and you should end up where you want to be, where you're meant to be.

CHARITY WORK

ONE OF THE BEST PARTS OF THE JOB has been the charity work I've been lucky enough to be a part of, particularly taking some sick kids down to the rink. You see their faces light up and you can't help but smile too.

I'd meet these kids at practice, give them a tour of the Saddledome, and they—I don't how else to put it—just shone.

Offhand, I remember one kid, from Medicine Hat, who was dying of cancer. Just a lovely, lovely young lad. So polite. Just tugged at your heart.

So he came in and I gave him all the tours. That night during the game, at the start of the third period, I tapped him on the shoulder and said, "Come with me." And I took him up into the press box, down the walkway, overtop of the clock to the other side of the arena where the broadcasters are all located.

I introduced him to everybody I could find. Our management, the guys who weren't playing from both teams, and of course everyone made quite a fuss over him. You should've seen his face…he was just speechless.

I'll never forget that. Ever. As long as I live. Him on that walkway, looking down on the players skating like little mice on the ice. Such a main event for him. For me too.

There are so many charities that need help. And they're all important. I try to help wherever, whenever I can, if I'm asked. One that's pretty dear to my heart, though, is the Organ Donors Society.

The various cancer charities too. I got to know a lot of the kids, like the little fella from Medicine Hat, and it was often very hard on me. I broke down quite a few times.

I got more into the charity end of things, of course, after I became a trainer. Then people started requesting that I do this and that, go to these dinners to speak and help with the auctions and things of that nature. And it's continued on, after I retired and I became an ambassador.

I wasn't a smart-aleck, I don't think. But I was very proud that I'd even be asked to help out.

DAN KROFFAT
Former pro wrestler, charity advocate, friend

I used to be involved in the world of entertainment, if you will. A way, way back.

I'd say Bearcat and I go back, oh, 30 years. We started running into each other at these charity golf tournaments and we found ourselves often talking about how we'd donate our time. I used to say I got a much more fulfilling feeling donating that time; that the paycheque is the success of the event. And that just lit him up.

We would travel to events, wherever, and never charged, as some people do. We bonded around that. When I retired in 1980, I thought to myself, *I need to find purpose in life.* I remember sitting with Bearcat having a coffee and telling him, "This volunteerism, this event-creating, this fund-raising, the philanthropic side of things certainly gives a person purpose." And he was really onboard with that. When I started running these golf tournaments—I've run 50 or 60 since I retired—he not once, never, said no.

What people should know, and celebrate, is that he's given thousands and thousands of hours and not been rewarded in a payment form. I've worked with a lot of celebrities and I get questions like, "Is the media going to be there?" Or, "Are the cameras going to be there?" *Hey, look at me, I'm a good guy.* They're playing the celebrity.

With Bearcat, that's never been the case. He isn't trying to be a celebrity. He just naturally is, because of his kindness and his generosity.

I used to work with and know lot of famous people when I was wrestling, in L.A. and places like that. A lot of people who were supposed to be "celebrities." And that sure diminished once you got to know that, yeah, on television you're one person but in reality you're another.

Bearcat has always been the real deal. Genuine. He has a very unique humility. He's personable, he's bubbly, he's friendly, but he's low-key. He doesn't push himself on people.

I do an event in Cochrane called the Community Builder Award, a tribute to an outstanding citizen. We started it about five years ago. One of those honourees, naturally, was Bearcat. It was the early stages of the event, so that one I ran myself. We really didn't have a committee then like we do today.

Well, we filled the room. We sold out the tickets.

He was from Okotoks. I was celebrating his contribution to the community there in another town, Cochrane. That didn't matter. The accolades that night, the things people had to say about him, were so on point that people would nod their heads. They knew.

There were no "Al Capone was a great guy, wonderful man" embellishments.

I used to say to Bearcat, "What I love is that every dime we raise is going toward the benefactor." No administrative cost, no celebrity cost.

That used to bring a smile to his face; part of what he needed to hear. He thinks about who he's helping when he's there, not just, "Oh, a free round of golf."

I think he has a great deal of sensitivity, of empathy. And I think we can all be envious of the relationship he has with his wife. He doesn't have his celebrity personality where she's sitting in the corner somewhere. When you see them, they're *together*.

I think he's a great example of who we all want to be. If you were going to pick someone as a mentor, I'd say Bearcat Murray would be a pretty darn good choice.

241

Well, holy cripes, when all these golf tournaments and charity events started up, everything just got crazy. I was popular because I was local, the trainer for the junior Centennials, the Cowboys, the Flames, and so on.

People talk about you donating your time…. You get a free dinner, free golf, everyone's happy to see you, and you're raising money for people who need it. It all fell into line. A heckuva good time.

You meet so many wonderful people becoming involved with charity initiatives. One of those people is Jerry Wood of Okotoks Ford-Lincoln. He's run a golf tournament here in Okotoks in support of Down syndrome for a long, long time. His daughter has Down syndrome. She's just a sweetheart. So we—Doug Barkley and I—would go to that tournament every year for, oh, 25 years, maybe 30. Jerry always treated you like a king. He's always been a great supporter of mine and in turn I've tried to help him out in any way I can.

The golf tournaments are an amazing way to raise money for charities and the people donating the money are happier'n hell to do it. I've been all over Western Canada at these things and the generosity is simply amazing.

BILL BROWN
Auctioneer, charity advocate, friend

Adding the auctioneering element onto his personality and his storytelling abilities at charity functions was a natural for Bearcat. I remember he came to one of our auto auctions, never having been to a truly big professional auction before, where we sell three or four cars every two minutes.

And his eyes…I'd never seen him surprised like that by anything before. He'd stayed for an hour or so, called me the next day, and said, "I *have* to learn how to do that."

Within five days he was practising. I got him some training tapes. It's unorthodox, he doesn't do it for living, but oh boy…it gave him another

window at charity events. Then all of a sudden, he told me he was getting four or five calls a week to do it.

His passion is incredible. I remember one event out in Okotoks, at the golf course there, Darcy Ranch, and I believe it was the first time I worked with him. When he got going, he was just unstoppable. And when he got to the part where he goes from auctioneer to yodeller, the crowd just ate it up. He entertained the living daylights out of them. There was this amazing energy in the room. Which he created.

They're laughing. They're happy. And when they're laughing and happy, they're spending more money. He was getting double the value of some stuff. I mean, I'm a third-generation auctioneer and I don't know if I could've got that kind of money.

So much of celebrity auctioneering is personality. And Bearcat, as everyone knows, has no shortage of that.

I'd known him a little bit before. Not well. But at that moment we became lifelong friends. And the thing is, he genuinely cares about the charities, about the community. Just a nice, nice guy. In all honesty, one of the nicest guys I've ever met.

In helping out, I'd use my connections to set up headliners for some of these events, popular players like Theoren Fleury. I had a desk calendar to keep track of everything and pretty soon each summer, June, July, August, September of that calendar were full, a golf tournament marked on it pret'near every day.

Holy mackerel. But where it's possible, I'm happy to help.

I just love talking to people. A favourite line of mine to wind up with when I'm at a function is, "I want to live to be 110 and then I want be shot by a jealous husband!"

I stole that from somebody. I admit it.

Well, one time I was out doing a speech at an old folks' home, west of the Saddledome, up in the hills. The residents of the home

were sitting in wheelchairs listening to me and then I came up with that line—"I want to live to be 110 and then I want to be shot by a jealous husband!"

And this lady who was sitting in the front row jumped up out of her wheelchair and said, "I hope it's mine!"

Well, I pret'near fainted dead away. What a great comeback. How cute is that?

The auctioneering is fun. We'd have someone's jersey that had been donated—going for $1,500 or $2,000—and I got to thinking, *Okay, how about I get this autographed?* Well, people went nuts. After we'd sold the thing, I'd take it back to the Dome, Morris Boyer was the trainer there then—a really good guy—and he'd get them autographed. I didn't have to go after the player at all. Just left it with Morris. I'd pick it up all signed and then I'd deliver it to the guy who bought it.

Well, those jerseys just kept bringing in more and more money. Incredible. One time I was wearing the jersey the Flames gave me to attend these events, with the number of the year I retired on the back, and I sold that. Anyway, I started talking and I got up to $1,500, so I stopped and said, "I gotta know who you want it signed by!" to know if I could get it done. Well, this guy stood up and said, "It's the jersey you're wearing that I'm bidding on! The one with BEARCAT on the back!"

So I signed it and gave it to him. But I was flabbergasted, I gotta tell ya.

One of the things that affects me most are the people in AA. I got involved with two Houses, Simon House being one of them. They've done a lot of really good work with people who are having drinking problems. Rob Laird set us up with that. They feed 'em there, they can live there; they really look after the guys, take them away from that lifestyle.

What really impressed me is when they had what they called a "birthday," which is an anniversary of when someone stopped drinking. Someone would go up there and say, "This is my 10th birthday." That

really got to my heart. Shirley and I, we'd be invited to the parties at the House in Bowness, and they'd get up and tell their stories and it really knocked you for a loop.

A lot of them were millionaires, very influential people. They'd be up there, crying, talking about how drinking wrecked their family, their marriage. Everything. Well, it got to me. For them to quit drinking, to defeat that, to me was an honest-to-goodness miracle.

To do something like that takes a very special kind of courage.

I mean, I drank…wine and such. Not to excess, but I liked to have a drink now and again. So I saw those people, what they're going through, how brave they are, and I started thinking, *What am I doing? Up here preaching and promoting not to drink, and here I am, a hypocrite.*

So it's been eight years since I had a drink.

You learn a lot. Those people are helping you every bit, probably more than you're helping them.

As I already mentioned, being interested in people, trying to help people, stretches all the way back to when I was a young kid during the Depression and the impact those guys who rode the boxcars looking for work had on me.

They'd come over our house, as I said, and my mom would feed them while I talked to them on the back step. Great people, just going through some hard times.

I really do think I just naturally like people because of the example my mom and dad set. If you think you can help somebody, try.

That's stayed with me all these years.

ROB LAIRD
Former RCMP officer, charity advocate, friend

I've known Bearcat since I moved to just outside Okotoks in 1980. I knew his dad, too, so he told me where the "Potlicker" name comes from. Jim, as Shirley calls him, has a heart of gold. I've done a lot of charity things

with a lot of people so I'm very picky and choosy who I corral, because you want to use their time wisely.

I've worked with people through all kinds of trials and tribulations, so I got Bearcat involved with an organization, Recovery Day, in Calgary. They hired me to help them raise $7 million to help build a couple facilities. One was a care centre for women. There are a lot for men, but very few for women, so I got Bear involved in that one. I told him, "We need to get one more guy involved in this. We need Lanny McDonald." So through Bearcat we met Lanny at the Marda Loop Starbucks in, oh, 2014. And through Bearcat, we got Lanny involved.

Bearcat knows everybody, right? So besides donating his time, he can help you get all these other people to lend their time.

He'll also do anything you need. In the summer of 2019, for example, I was part of a fundraising event called River Trust to help raise money for the healthcare system out here in the Foothills area. So, naturally, I got in touch with Bearcat, to put him in a 10,000 horsepower dragster—meaning there's more horsepower in that one car than all the cars that go around the track at the Daytona 500. We got the dragster through an organization called Dark Side Racing, run by a lady named Kelly Fedorowich, the fastest woman in Canada.

So we put Bearcat, wearing earmuffs, in this dragster—jacked up off the ground—and we lowered him into the cockpit. And they fired this dragster up, flames shooting out all over the place, this thing really humming, and Bearcat's eyes got as big as saucers, let me tell you. He thought, "Holy cow!"

We dropped a whole bunch of celebrities, including Bret "The Hitman" Hart, in that cockpit. All for a good cause. Including Bearcat.

He was excited about that—getting in *and* getting out.

Call from the Hall

GOING INTO THE HOCKEY HALL OF FAME IN 2009, after being absolutely thrilled out of my mind just to get the Flames job in the first place, by pure luck really, is something I really, honestly can't put into words.

And if you ask anyone who knows me even a little bit, they'll tell you I'm never at a loss for words.

If you're lucky enough for something like that to happen to you, it makes you think back to all the things that happened during your career—the people you met, the friends you made, winning the Stanley Cup, the wins and the losses, the highs and the lows.

All of it. Every bit.

And my god, you should've seen my dad. To have him, the original Bearcat, the person most responsible for me being in that position in the first place, there to share it with me was something I never could've imagined. He was so proud, it just boggled my mind.

It was really funny to watch him. And all the guys treated him so great. He'd always been treated great. But that's way hockey people are.

Over the years, he'd attend all our home games and come down to the dressing room afterward—but only if we won, never if we lost. If we lost, he'd just go home. He'd be outside the room, then one of the guys would bring him in, arm around his shoulders, and would holler

over at me, "Bearcat, you've got a visitor!" I'd look up and there Dad would be, great big grin. So you can image how excited he was that I was going into the Hall of Fame.

They put up a plaque for you, at the Professional Hockey Athletic Trainers Society/Society of Professional Hockey Equipment Managers' Hall of Fame display located inside the training room area upstairs in the Hall, and you're there. Forever.

Being honoured in that way is something you never imagine could happen. Not in a million years.

My buddy, the guy who really ran the thing, was an assistant trainer with Buffalo. When I first heard that I was in the running, he called me up and told me he was getting all the votes tallied up and, yeah, it looked like I'd be going in.

Thing is, a lot of the current trainers didn't really know me. This is, remember, quite a while after I'd retired. But my friend, he said, "I filled 'em in pretty damn quick about all that you've done!"

Seemed as if he did a pretty job talking me up, because I was voted in 100 per cent. Unanimous.

I went into the Hall the same year John Davidson did for broadcasting, which was great, so special, J.D. and I having spent that time together with the Centennials and being such good friends. We'd known each such other a long time it seemed only fitting, somehow.

Another big thrill, and a real surprise, was that Danny Gare had heard the news on the radio about me being inducted into the Hall of Fame, so he jumped in his car and drove to Toronto from Buffalo for the big day.

I was sitting there in the room with Shirley—had no idea he'd decided to drive up—and suddenly there was this tap on the shoulder. I turned around, and there was Danny. Well, I just went crazy, I was so happy.

Pret'near a perfect day, all in all.

DANNY GARE
Calgary Centennials, 1971–74

I came there as a 17-year-old and Bearcat was always helpful, embracing, do anything to help you out—equipment-wise or whatever you needed.

Wasn't often he got upset, but when he did you didn't want to be on the receiving end because he some growl in him, the little potlicker.

He did everything. Drove the bus, for instance. I remember one time we were on a Western trip, Winnipeg, Saskatoon, heading up to Brandon then north to Flin Flon. Long trip and it was cold as s—t. Wasn't the best bus in the world, either, very little heat, this and that.

"Well, we were on our way to Flin Flon and the friggin' bus broke down. It was snowing, minus-whatever, icy roads, day off, and we were driving in. We were, I don't know, maybe four or five miles out. So Bearcat told us to get out and we pushed this bus to the top of a hill. All the players.

Then we coasted into town. And there's Bearcat at the wheel, like the pilot of a plane, guiding us into Flin Flon. Not that we really gave two s—ts about getting into Flin Flon.

Afterward, you'd turned pro and he'd always be calling to see how you were doing, still looking out for you. I'd see him, Shirley, and little Bear sometimes in the off-season when I went home to Nelson. Like a big brother to you, if you need to talk to somebody.

I see him on Facebook sometimes and I think of how he helped me get to where I did. Not just me. A number of others, and not just the amateur ranks but the professional ranks, too.

What an ambassador for the game. Just an amazing individual, family man, father. And a genuine trainer, my very first. They're all good. Not too many bad trainers.

But to me, he fit the mould for the job in all categories.

When he was inducted into the Hall of Fame, it was so well-deserved and long overdue, in my opinion. I drove up from Buffalo to be there and wouldn't have missed it for the world.

Being Bearcat

I'M 88 NOW AND EVERY DAY I think back on what's happened to me during my life, where I came from to what I've been able to experience, it just floors me.

I honestly wake up every morning and shake my head. Crazy. Absolutely crazy.

I think back to how it all started, when Cec first came after me to be his trainer. Well, I'd quit that really good job because the company wanted me to go back to Estevan and I was working for Shirley's uncle Bill in the fairground setup at Bowness Park. John Hextall, the original owner, did not come back from the war. He was killed in action, but he had big plans for the property and the City of Calgary took it over after he died. So Bill basically designed and upgraded it to what it is today. The merry-go-round and Ferris wheel that were at Bowness for decades were later donated by Bill to Heritage Park. And they're still there. Still operational.

Anyway, Bill said, "Why don't you come and run the concessions for me at Bowness?" So I did. Well, I had a helluva time. I had suggested to him that we set up skating in the park in the wintertime with a big fire pit. People will have a helluva time, I told him, they'll come out like a darn. He didn't see it; just too busy doing the rides and stuff, I guess. Turns out the city used the idea later and it was a big hit.

Well, then Cec came to see me, and we went and visited out back, in the woods—probably had a beer or two—and he said, "Bear, I need you to be my trainer. We've bought this hockey team…" We talked under this tree that is still there today and considered a heritage asset. Planted by Mr. Hextall.

Well, bingo. History.

All these years later, people—people my age, young people, all kinds of people—still recognize me and want to talk to me. Still ask me how I got the name Bearcat. I've been asked that about a million times.

Everybody always asks, "Who was your favourite player?" They mention Lanny, of course. But I always say, "They were all my favourite." And I'm not lying.

Sure, sometimes you argue with people or don't hit it off or don't get along from time to time. I understood, they were worried about their health, their careers, so sometimes you'd get into it a bit.

But I don't think I had a problem, a *real* problem, with anybody in all my life as a trainer. I loved everybody—except one guy. And I won't name him now. Just didn't work out; we didn't get along. One of those things.

And, of course, people also still want to know about winning the Cup, that night, doing it in Montreal. All that. Little did I know. Little could I have imagined. Who would have any idea any of this could happen to a guy like me?

I certainly have no explanation.

I just walk down the street and people who weren't even born when I was working as a trainer say to me, "Hiya, Bearcat!" I go to an event and I'm swamped.

Why? That's something I'm continually asking myself. Why me? I'm just a snot-nosed, scrawny little guy. I'm a distinctive-looking potlicker, I guess, but there's nothing special about me. For some reason, though, I'm considered an icon.